Integrating Math Into the Early Childhood Classroom

JOAN D. MARTIN & VICKI C. MILSTEIN

New York • Toronto • London • Auckland • Sydney
Mexico City • New Delhi • Hong Kong • Buenos Aires

Teaching
Resources

Dedicated to
Kim and Kate Milstein, and Austin, Ben, and Joe Martin, our children,
who at a young age introduced both of us to the very personal nature of teaching.
—J. D. M. and V. C. M.

Thank you to
The early childhood, kindergarten, and primary teachers of the
Brookline and Newton Public Schools, for their interest in supporting current
research as it applies to mathematics education

The educators of Wheelock College, Education Department
and Boston College, Mathematics Institute

Our families, for their understanding and support through
the messy process of exploring mathematics materials for use in our
courses, classrooms, and presentations

Special thanks to Amelia Klein at Wheelock College, Fr. Stanley Bezsuzka,
S. J. and Margaret J. Kenney at Boston College Mathematics Institute, and
Leo G. Martin, who are important to us both personally and professionally

Edited by Joan Novelli.
Cover design by Brian LaRossa.
Cover photo by James Levin.
Back cover photos by Leo G. Martin.
Interior design by Diana Fitter and Holly Grundon.
Interior art by Cary Pillo, Maxie Chambliss, and James Hale.
ISBN–13: 978-0-439-58059-5
ISBN–10: 0-439-58059-5

Contents

About Math in a PreK–K Classroom

How to Use This Book 4

What the Research Says 5

Math Rich . . . Language Rich 6

100 Math Words to Use 8

Assessment and Record Keeping. 9

Connections to the Math Standards
and Curriculum Focal Points 9

Bibliography 11

Reproducible Templates and Forms . . 12

Math Around the Room

Standards Connections Chart 14

Strategies and Activities for
Integrating Math. 15

Reproducible Templates and Forms . . 22

Rituals and Routines

Standards Connections Chart 25

Strategies and Activities for
Integrating Math. 26

Reproducible Templates and Forms . . 37

Sensory Explorations

Standards Connections Chart 41

Strategies and Activities for
Integrating Math. 42

Reproducible Templates and Forms . . 51

Block Center

Standards Connections Chart 53

Strategies and Activities for
Integrating Math. 54

Reproducible Templates and Forms . . 66

Dramatic Play

Standards Connections Chart 69

Strategies and Activities for
Integrating Math. 70

Reproducible Templates and Forms . . 84

Art Activities

Standards Connections Chart 90

Strategies and Activities for
Integrating Math. 91

Cooking Activities

Standards Connections Chart 99

Strategies and Activities for
Integrating Math. 100

Reproducible Templates and Forms. . 108

Movement and Outdoor Activities

Standards Connections Chart 110

Strategies and Activities for
Integrating Math. 111

Home-School Connections

Standards Connections Chart 119

Strategies and Activities for
Integrating Math. 120

Reproducible Templates and Forms. . 121

About Math in a PreK–K Classroom

Our world is rich in numbers and children learn the concept of numbers every day in informal ways. It is a young child who notices the bigger cookie or the person who has "more." It is a young child who explores size, trying to fit all kinds of items into a container. Children try out their new knowledge in interesting and important ways. A child telling a teacher that his recipe for cake includes "four inches of sugar" offers us a striking example of the use of the vocabulary of standard measurement. We can tell a lot about this child's emerging understanding as we appreciate the use of words in this context. The chance to ask a child to "show me how much that is" becomes a rich anecdotal assessment of developing understanding.

Teachable moments are everywhere and occur naturally throughout a child's day. The increased use of math language in early childhood classrooms will lead to increased opportunities for children to make that language a part of their own understanding. In that way we help children talk about the "big ideas" without getting lost in the meaning of unfamiliar words. Going on a "hexagon hunt" or working out a solution to a complex puzzle helps children understand and strategize. That is the goal of this book—to provide materials and strategies that develop young children's ability to understand a problem and the resources to solve it.

How to Use This Book

This book is designed with the typical prekindergarten and kindergarten classroom in mind, with lessons that build on routines that are part of an ordinary day. Use the materials in this book to actively plan for the teachable moments that are part of these routines to create an environment that supports meaningful mathematical learning. Encouraging children to express their reasoning or to explain the way in which a problem-solving plan might work is an important part of these everyday lessons.

The book begins with set-up suggestions for a math-rich classroom, followed by strategies for promoting math discoveries during daily rituals and routines, such as attendance and lunch count. From there, you'll find ideas

". . . throughout development, before and after entrance to school, children are normally exposed to physical and social environments rich in mathematical opportunities. Children encounter quantity in the physical world, counting numbers in the social world, and mathematical ideas in the literary world."

(Ginsburg, 1993)

for math explorations that relate to sensory table explorations, block building, dramatic play experiences, art and cooking activities, and outdoor play. You can use these suggestions and strategies in whatever order you choose—selecting those that best meet the needs, interests, and abilities of your students. Because children benefit from repetition, be sure to revisit activities. The familiarity children experience will boost their confidence, and allow them to make fresh observations and develop both new and deeper understandings.

What the Research Says

By the time young children are ready for preschool or kindergarten, they've already developed a wealth of mathematical knowledge through their everyday experiences. They notice "equal sharing" when cutting a favorite dessert. They learn sorting when organizing doll clothes, toy cars, and play dishes and cups. Children who help set a table or pass out markers learn one-to-one correspondence; they develop concepts related to counting when they empty grocery bags, go up and down stairs, or ask to read "just one more book."

Experts agree that preschoolers have significant mathematical strengths. "In particular, it appears that young children—despite important limitations—are capable of understanding much more about number and arithmetic than previously or commonly thought possible" (Baroody, 2003).

What does this mean for the early childhood classroom? "Research indicates that better mathematics education can and should begin early. Research shows that higher quality programs result in learning benefits into elementary school, including in mathematics" (Clements, Sarama, & DiBiase, 2003).

To make math a part of their lives, young children need to feel comfortable in the world of number, quantity, measurement, shape, and design. This cannot be accomplished through "math time" alone. Math learning must occur throughout the day, embedded in the authentic experiences children encounter through classroom routines, play, and active learning. As children use math they will begin to see themselves as capable in a world of numbers. This confidence and a strong foundation in understanding the way numbers work will give our students their best chance at success with more challenging material in later grades. Teachers need to explore math with their students, making it an opportunity to learn through manipulating objects, trying a strategy, or asking a new question. Celebrating children's efforts will encourage their continued interest in the use of numbers in their lives. We must strive to hear all children reflect that they are good at math and proud of their accomplishments.

This book is designed to support teachers in implementing research-based mathematical learning in prekindergarten and kindergarten programs, in ways that honor both the child's need to explore and discover and the child's ability to develop essential mathematical understandings. As teachers, it is in our power to make math integral to the child's emerging understanding of the world. From counting to problem solving, geometry to measurement, math opportunities abound. Now these opportunities can become the basis for the creation of math-rich environments in our early childhood classrooms. The joy of sharing in their developing skills will make this exploration an engaging one for all of us who teach our youngest students.

Math-Rich . . . Language-Rich

For children to solidify their understanding in mathematics, they must first become familiar with and then competent in their understanding and use of mathematical language. Some explicit teaching may need to be a part of this process, and the regular use of mathematical language will need to be a part of every teacher's daily interaction with children.

Before cooking, for example, a teacher can explicitly demonstrate the use of measuring cups. Initially, simply pointing out that the cups are different sizes will suffice. As children become familiar with the concept that a ¼-cup-size measuring cup holds less than a ½-cup-size measuring cup, more complex concepts can be introduced. At cleanup time, organizing the cups from smallest to largest will give children a chance to build an association between the names and the actual cup sizes.

Math Talk

Throughout this book, you'll find suggestions and conversation prompts, based on specific activities, for encouraging understanding and use of language related to math. Use these as starting-off points, adapting the ideas to work with what's going on in your classroom. On pages 22–23, you'll also find reproducible cards with sample discussion starters, perfect for keeping on hand as you observe children's work in key areas (including shapes, sorting, graphing, and number lines).

Teaching
Tip

For guidelines
related to areas of
mathematical focus
at the preK–K level
(which will inform
choices related
to mathematical
language), check
*Curriculum
Focal Points for
Prekindergarten
Through Grade 8
Mathematics: A Quest
for Coherence*
(NCTM, 2006).

When talking about geometry, one of the curriculum focal points of math instruction in the preK–K classroom, there is general agreement that the names of the basic shapes are important. But it is also important for teachers to notice with children that a triangle is a triangle no matter what perspective or orientation it is. Many children believe that a shape is a triangle only when it is equilateral or isosceles with the vertex (point) at the top and one side oriented horizontally on the bottom. If you turn the triangle, some children may feel less sure of its name. Noticing opportunities to incorporate math language into different situations encourages children to try out terminology they're learning and add to their understanding.

Graphing is a delightful experience for children, and another example of an opportunity to naturally incorporate mathematical language. As children count and compare data on a graph, they can use terms such as *more than, less than, equal,* and *unequal* to articulate observations and demonstrate their growing knowledge.

Everyday conversations in preK–K classrooms are opportunities to build language for mathematical understandings. Children naturally love language, and learning new words to describe what they see in the world around them not only builds on their mathematical understandings, it is a big confidence booster.

100 Math Words to Use

Following are 100 words that are appropriate for use in a preK–K classroom:

Above	Heavy (heavier, heaviest)	Quarter
After	Height	Rectangle
Alike	Hexagon	Rhombus
Around	High (higher, highest)	Same
Before	Horizontal	Second
Behind	Hour	Shape
Below	In front of	Short (shorter, shortest)
Big (bigger, biggest)	Last	Size
Bottom	Length	Small (smaller, smallest)
Calendar	Less (than)	Sort (sorting)
Circle	Light (lighter, lightest)	Square
Compare	Line	Straight
Cone	Long (longer, longest)	Symmetrical
Cube	Low (lower, lowest)	Table
Curve	Many	Tall (taller, tallest)
Cylinder	Measure(ment)	Third
Date	Minute	Through
Day	Month	Time
Diagonal	More (than)	Today
Different	Next to	Tomorrow
Dime	Nickel	Top
Direction	Not equal (to)	Trapezoid
Dollar	Number	Triangle
Ellipse	Numeral	Turn
Equal (to)	Octagon	Under
Estimate	Once	Unequal
Few	Oval	Vertical
Fifth	Over	Weigh (weight)
First	Part	Whole
Flip	Pattern	Width
Fourth	Penny	Year
Graph	Pentagon	Yesterday
Greater (than)	Prism	
Half	Problem	

Assessment and Record Keeping

A systematic use of data is important to adequately assess progress. Record keeping should come from authentic experiences during play or discoveries expressed in conversation throughout the day. Questioning a child one-on-one, out of context, will often reflect the child's comfort level with the format of assessment rather than his or her true understanding.

Two ready-to-use assessment and record-keeping forms are included on pages 12–13. The first, an assessment checklist, allows you to identify the skills you wish to observe and assess, and to customize the chart according to those needs. The second provides a framework for assessments or records for a selected project or activity. This record sheet is appropriate for use with portfolio projects. Consider attaching a photo to the record sheet for those projects that are not permanent (such as block construction) or those that don't fit in a file folder (such as artwork). You can use these record sheets as they are or modify them to meet your classroom needs.

Connections to the Math Standards and Curriculum Focal Points

The National Council of Teachers of Mathematics (NCTM) has outlined learning expectations for grades preK–12 in *Principles and Standards for School Mathematics* (2000). The NCTM's *Curriculum Focal Points for Prekindergarten Through Grade 8 Mathematics: A Quest for Coherence* (2006) builds on the learning expectations outlined in the standards, identifying three focal points, and providing descriptions of key concepts and skills at each grade level. A "Connections" section for each grade incorporates additional topics in meaningful ways, sometimes making connections to focal points for a previous grade (allowing students to reinforce and extend their understanding) and other times introducing concepts that are part of the focal points at the next grade. Together, the focal points and connections support a curriculum that provides students with "a connected, coherent, ever expanding body of mathematical knowledge and ways of thinking" (NCTM, 2006).

For grades preK–K, the three key focal points, or recommended areas of content emphasis, are Number and Operations, Geometry, and Measurement, with an emphasis on providing a context in instruction that promotes the process standards identified in *Principles and Standards for School Mathematics*

Standards Connections

Activity	Number and Operations	Algebra	Geometry	Measurement	Data Analysis
Chants and Patterns	•	•	•		•
Presenting the Count and Countess!	•	•	•		•
Morning Meeting Survey Plates	•	•			•
Calendar Connections	•	•		•	•
Calendar Count-Up/Countdown	•	•		•	
Double-Chain Discoveries	•	•	•	•	•
From One to Five	•	•			
Snack Table Centerpieces	•	•			•
Tickets, Please	•		•		•
Napkins and Numbers	•	•	•		
Snack Mat Math	•	•	•	•	•
Raisin Box Investigations	•		•	•	•
I Spy Snacks		•	•		
The Snack Count, and Countess	•				
Cookie Count	•	•			
Do We Have Enough?	•	•		•	
Snack Graphs	•	•		•	•

Teaching Tip

A chart detailing specific standards connections for each activity appears on the first page of each section of this book (pages 14, 25, 41, 53, 69, 90, 99, 110, and 119).

Teaching Tip

For more information about NCTM math standards and curriculum focal points, visit www.nctm.org.

(communication, reasoning, representation, connections, and problem solving). Additionally, the guidelines incorporate important connections to Data Analysis and Algebra to support children in building understandings across the standards.

What does this look like in a preK–K classroom? Consider an everyday experience: snack time. As children set the table, they count and use one-to-one correspondence to make sure there's a napkin and cup at each place (supporting the curriculum focal points for Number and Operations but with an opportunity to use Data Analysis to support it). Place mats at their table may give children an opportunity to explore aspects of measurement if the mats have lines of different lengths on them. Children can measure their crackers or carrot sticks to see which is longer or taller. By implementing instructional goals in context, you provide meaningful opportunities for children to develop understanding.

In order to tie assessment and record keeping to the appropriate topics, each section in this book begins with a standards chart that outlines specific content standards connections for each activity. (See pages 14, 25, 41, 53, 69, 90, 99, 110, and 119.) When planning and guiding instructional experiences, engaging students in mathematical conversations, and assessing student learning, keep in mind that most preK–K children are at the initial stages of these expectations.

As teachers, our belief in the value of the process of mathematics will encourage children to take risks, make a plan, adapt a strategy, and explain their ideas. If children believe that they are "good at math," their exploration will lead them to deeper understanding, and we all have an investment in making their mathematical understanding an enduring strength.

Bibliography

Baroody, A. (2004). The role of psychological research in the development of early childhood mathematics standards. In D. H. Clements, J. Sarama & A. DiBiase (Eds.), *Engaging young children in mathematics: Standards for early childhood mathematics education.* (pp. 149-172). Mahwah, N.J.: Lawrence Erlbaum Associates.

Clements, D. H., (1999). Geometric and spatial thinking in young children. In J. V. Copley (Ed.), *Mathematics in the early years.* (pp. 66-79). Reston, VA: National Council of Teachers of Mathematics.

Clements, D. H., (1999). "Concrete" manipulatives, concrete ideas. *Contemporary Issues in Early Childhood, 1*(1), 45-60.

Ginsburg, H. P. & Baron, J. (1993). Cognition: Young children's construction of mathematics. In R. J. Jensen (Ed.), *Research ideas for the classroom: Early childhood mathematics* (pp. 3-21). New York: Macmillan.

Graham, T. A., Nash, C., & Paul, K. (1997). Young children's exposure to mathematics: The child care context. *Early Childhood Education Journal, 25*(1), 31-38.

National Council of Teachers of Mathematics. (2006). *Curriculum focal points for prekindergarten through grade 8 mathematics.* Reston, VA: National Council of Teachers of Mathematics.

National Council of Teachers of Mathematics. (2000). *Principles and standards for school mathematics.* Reston, VA: National Council of Teachers of Mathematics.

Nicol, C. & Crespo, S., (2005). Exploring mathematics in imaginary places: Rethinking what counts as meaningful contexts for learning mathematics. *School Science and Mathematics, 105*(5), 240-251.

Richardson, K., (2004). Making sense. In D. H. Clements, J. Sarama & A. DiBiase (Eds.), *Engaging young children in mathematics: Standards for early childhood mathematics education.* (pp. 321-324). Mahwah, N.J.: Lawrence Erlbaum Associates.

Sarama, J. & Clements, D. H., (2004). Building blocks for early childhood mathematics, *Early Childhood Research Quarterly, 19,* 181-189.

Shilling, W. A., (2002). Mathematics, music, and movement: Exploring concepts and connections. *Early Childhood Education Journal, 29*(31), 179-184.

Varol, F. and Farran, D. C., (2006). Early mathematical growth: How to support young children's mathematical development. *Early Childhood Education Journal, 33*(6), 381-387.

Name _____ Date _____

Assessment Checklist

Skills	Skill Mastered	Skill at Emergent Level	Skill Not Yet Demonstrated

Student's Level of Independence	Skill Mastered	Skill at Emergent Level	Skill Not Yet Demonstrated
Able to begin to develop a plan			
Develops a plan appropriate to the problem			
Expresses Ideas			
Is flexible when working through a problem			

Integrating Math Into the Early Childhood Classroom Scholastic Teaching Resources

Name _____ **Date** _____

Portfolio Records

Activity/Project Name: _____

Target Area: _____

Skills Demonstrated:

   Individually: _____

   _____

   _____

   _____

   _____

   Cooperatively: _____

   _____

   _____

   _____

   _____

Anecdotal Notes:_____

_____

_____

_____

_____

_____

_____

Math Around the Room

Standards Connections					
Activity	Number and Operations	Algebra	Geometry	Measurement	Data Analysis
Attendance Board/Graphs	•	•			•
Daily Schedule	•	•		•	
Lunch Count	•	•			•
Wall Graph	•	•			•
Roll-Out Graph	•	•	•	•	•
Song Charts	•	•	•	•	
Numeral and Shape Posters	•		•		
Inventory Day Sorting Mat	•	•	•	•	•

Take a look around a "typical" preK–K classroom. Do you see math tools neatly organized and labeled? Are graphs, charts, and number lines at children's eye level? The right materials invite the kinds of mathematical explorations that build a foundation for more complex understandings. Here's how to set up a classroom that naturally integrates math into the day—from attendance boards to song charts.

Math Tools

The following list consists of items that invite math exploration and discovery in preK–K classrooms. Thinking aloud about and modeling the use of the materials will help children both with developing problem-solving strategies and with matching appropriate tools to needs/situations.

- Adding machine tape (and/or string/ribbon for measuring)
- Attribute blocks
- Balance (pan and bucket)
- Beads
- Blocks (such as unit, large hollow, solid 3-D, arch, prisms, pyramids, cone, hemispheres, and parquetry blocks)
- Calendars (not necessarily to be used daily)
- Clipboards
- Clocks
- Collections of small items (for example, toy cars and animals, buttons)
- Counters
- Counting wand (see page 28)
- Craft sticks
- Dice
- Dominoes
- Dot paper
- Geoboards
- Graph board (for attendance and "voting")
- Kitchen supplies (dishes, utensils, and pots in labeled bins)
- Legos
- Links
- Measuring cups and teaspoons (organized and displayed by size)
- Money (play)

- Name Tags (for graphing)
- Number cards/charts
- Number lines (horizontal and vertical to 20)
- Numeral cards
- Paper
- Pattern blocks
- Plastic bottles, cups, and containers (sorted into labeled bins)
- Play clay utensils
- Playing cards
- Puzzles/games
- Roll-out graph
- Scales
- Shape cards and/or posters
- Sorting trays/mats
- Spinners
- Student record sheets (such as tally sheets, graphing sheets, and ten frame sheets)
- Teddy bear counters
- Ten frames (see page 40)
- Thermometer
- Timer
- Unifix cubes (for measuring and for problem solving, especially around "voting" results)
- Unit blocks (organized by shape and size)
- Whiteboards
- Yarn (and/or ribbon, string)

Teaching Tip

Be sure to let children see when a problem is not solved with the first try. It is important to develop the ability to be a risk taker and nothing ensures that with more efficiency than watching a teacher in the process.

Teaching Tip

Permanently display a vertical and a horizontal number line in the room. Each number line should go up to at least the numeral 10, just enough to see the effect of the move to two digits. It is important that the numerals on the vertical number line are written so that digits in the ones place are aligned.

Attendance Board

An attendance board is a great way to introduce young children with limited mathematical backgrounds to the idea of organization of data. Set up a simple attendance board as follows:

1. Divide the attendance board (this can be a foam board tacked up to the back of a short bookcase, a cabinet, or a wall) into two columns (left and right).

2. In the column on the left, draw a sad face and write "I am not here."

3. In the column on the right, side draw a happy face and write "I am here."

4. Place a class set of Velcro dots on each side of the attendance board.

5. To make a class set of name tags, glue each child's photo to foam board and trim to size. Write the child's name on his or her tag.

6. As children enter the classroom each day, they move their name tags from the "I am not here" side to the "I am here" side.

Attendance Graphs

Vary the attendance board routine by setting up the attendance board as a graph.

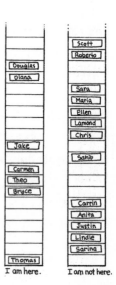

- For the simplest graphing experience, begin with a vertical attendance graph (see illustration, right) with two bars labeled "I am here." "I am not here." To begin, all counters (name tags) are placed on the "I am not here" bar. As children arrive, they move their counters to the "I am here" bar. In this way, they see the graph take shape as each child checks in. Use the visual organization of the counters (without counting them) to compare data. Ask: *Are there more children here or not here? How can you tell?*

- Once children are comfortable exploring the data visually, use the same graph to count up and find out how many children are "here" and "not here."

- Later, include numbers alongside the graph (see illustration, right) so children can make a connection to the last number stated (for example, 15 and all the people up to 15 are here—15 is inclusive of all the numbers up to it). Begin to get into "counting on." Start at the number that represents how many children are absent (assuming there are fewer children absent than present), then count on to find out how many more are here. (For more information on teaching with the attendance board, see page 26.)

16

Daily Schedule

Often classrooms display a vertical schedule with uniform boxes starting at the top for the beginning of the day and continuing to the bottom for the end of the day. Such a schedule lists activities in order, the time of day for each, and perhaps a clock showing the time of each event. To help young children begin to build concepts of time, display a horizontal schedule. Such a schedule follows the same organization as reading, which reinforces concepts of print for children, such as left-to-right orientation. When creating and using such a schedule, keep the following in mind:

1. Make sure that the size of each section of the schedule reflects the amount of time spent in the activity. This provides children with a visual "picture" of time and encourages understanding.

2. Notice the different-sized schedule blocks with children and point out that some are bigger and some are smaller, reflecting that the amount of time they spend on some activities will be more or less than on other activities.

3. As children begin to associate the block of time they spend with each part of the daily schedule, they'll make connections to the varying sizes of the boxes on the schedule and begin to develop concepts of time accordingly.

Greeting and Morning Meeting	Calendar	Choice Time	Outdoor Recess	Snack	Read Aloud & Literacy	Special Projects	Lunch	Rest Time	Math	Recess	Daily News	Dismissal
									$1 + 1 = 2$			
8:15–8:30	8:30–8:45	8:45–10:00	10:00–10:30	10:30–10:45	10:45–11:15	11:15–12:00	12:00–12:30	12:30–1:00	1:00–1:30	1:30–2:00	2:00–2:15	2:15–2:30

"Math Talk"

Use the daily schedule as a springboard for conversations that incorporate math language and concepts:

- What happens first (second, third, and so on) in our day?

- If someone was looking for us during the middle part of our day, where do you think we could be found? How do you know this?

- What do you think you'll spend the most time doing today? How can you tell?

- Are there parts of our day that take up about the same amount of time? What can you tell me about this?

- If you could add more time to one part of our day, what would it be? What section of this schedule would it take up?

Lunch Count

In programs where students must designate their lunch plan each day, provide reusable graphs to record choices.

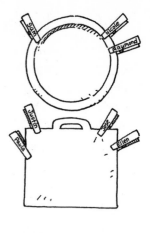

1. Write each child's name on a spring-type clothespin. (Use permanent or paint markers.) Place the clothespins in a basket.

2. Label a large, sturdy paper or plastic plate "School Lunch." Label a lunch box cutout "Lunch Box."

3. Place the clothespins and the lunch count plate and lunch box in the attendance board area.

4. Have children clip their clothespins to the plate or lunch box to indicate their choices.

5. To reinforce a connection between numerals and the quantities they represent, display the numeral that represents the total for each lunch choice. (Write numerals on index cards and clip to the corresponding graphs.) This is a valuable daily activity for reinforcing double-digit numerals, which can be challenging for young children.

6. Have the class "Count/Countess" for the day (see page 28) report on the lunch numbers (along with attendance numbers) during group or Morning Meeting time.

Wall Graph

Reusable graphs invite spontaneous data collection and are ready to use for more formal investigations.

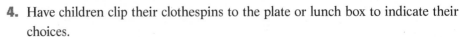

1. Use foam board to set up the graph. A dark-color board works well for a graph with self-stick labels to designate numbered spaces.

2. Place a Velcro dot at the bottom of each column. Place Velcro dots on the back of index cards and keep these handy for labeling the graph.

3. There are several options for making graph markers. If you're using a two-column chart to record Yes/No votes or a similar survey with two response choices (for example, "Do you want indoor or outdoor recess today?"), children can use spring-type clothespins to record their answers. They simply clip their clothespin to the side that corresponds to their response. Or make graph markers by writing children's names on name-tag-size pieces of foam board. Place a Velcro dot on the back of each. Place a Velcro dot in the center of each numbered space, as well, so children can easily record their vote or response to any graph question.

Roll-Out Graph

Roll-out graphs are easy to store and, because of their giant size, fun to use. To store, simply roll it up. Use these graphs to collect data—for example, at the dramatic play center, graph inventories of all the fruits and vegetables in the kitchen area, or shoes at the "shoe shop." (See page 76 for more information.) For a seasonal connection, graph the number of mittens/gloves/hats on the first cold school day. (See page 112 for more information.)

1. Make a roll-out graph with white contact paper (leave the backing on). You can also use wallpaper in different colors (ask for leftover rolls at a home-goods store). Windowpane-checked wallpaper provides built-in graph squares. Laminate wallpaper for durability (or look for the washable type).

2. Cut the contact paper or wallpaper into long strips. Use permanent markers (or narrow colorful tape, such as electrical tape) to create a row of 20 boxes on each (see illustration, below).

3. When you want to use this graph, have children work together to roll it out. Weights on the corners will keep the graph flat on the floor. For labels, use sticky notes at the base of each graph strip.

4. Use the graphs to give children a visual representation of data. For example, to sort and graph blocks used in a structure, set out as many graph strips as there are block shapes. Label each strip to represent a block shape. Let children sort the blocks onto the corresponding strips.

Teaching Tip

Children's sorting activities lend themselves well to graphing experiences. For example, children might sort their name cards into two groups as follows: "I like pizza" and "I don't like pizza." Use a follow-up graph to encourage flexible thinking about subgroups: For children who like pizza, what kind do they like best? Graphing experiences such as these encourage understanding of inclusive and exclusive sets.

" Math Talk "

Use children's observations of their roll-out graph data to reinforce math language for comparisons:

- How many more rectangular blocks than cylindrical blocks did you use?

- Which two shapes did you use the same number of for your structure?

- Did you use more of the triangles or the circles? How can you tell?

- Which shape do you think was most important in your structure? Why?

Teaching Tip

For favorite counting songs, chants, and finger plays, try the following resources:

Juba This and Juba That by Virginia Tashian (Little Brown, 1995)

Math for the Very Young: A Handbook of Activities for Parents and Teachers by Lydia Polonsky, Dorothy Freedman, Susan Lesher, and Kate Morrison (John Wiley, 1995)

Sing Along and Learn: Marvelous Math (with audio CD) by Ken Sheldon (Scholastic, 2001)

Song Charts

Charts for songs, chants, and finger plays give teachers a chance to review and reinforce mathematical language in engaging and interactive ways. Numerals, number words, and pictures of basic math quantities (for example, five duck pictures for the song "Five Little Ducks") are all useful in helping children make math connections through these daily interactions. Following are tips for making the most of these charts:

1. When creating song, chant, or finger play charts, use a different-color marker to highlight number words. Place sticker dots corresponding to the quantity next to these words to provide visual cues. This also reinforces subitizing skills (the ability to recognize the number of objects in a set without actually counting the objects; see page 10).

2. As a variation, write the words to songs, chants, and finger plays on sentence strips and place them in a pocket chart. Provide corresponding picture cards for children to manipulate as they recite the words.

Numeral and Shape Posters

Invite children to help create numeral and shape posters with colorful paints and collage materials. The block area is a good place to display these posters, as children will be encouraged to use the number and shape vocabulary in context as they build various structures.

1. Write numerals and number words on sheets of sturdy paper (or cardstock)—one numeral/number word per sheet. Let children illustrate the numerals to show how many each represents. For example, to illustrate the numeral 1, a child might glue on one cupcake holder, or paint a picture of one heart. For 2, a child might glue on two cotton balls or stamp two stars.

2. To create a set of shape posters, draw a picture and write the name of that shape on the paper (for example, a drawing of a square and the word "square"). Let children illustrate the shapes with their own drawings or paintings, or with pictures from magazines in which they see those shapes. While children may not be at a stage where they understand, for example, what makes one quadrilateral different from another, it's helpful to encourage exploration and understanding of the properties of these shapes, in addition to the use of shape names in meaningful contexts.

3. Children can make their own set of cards to match the shape and numeral posters at school and take them home to learn more with their families. Include a note with the cards suggesting ways families can use them to reinforce learning at home—for example, by displaying them and inviting their children to notice shapes (or numerals) around the home that are the same as the ones on their cards.

Inventory Day Sorting Mat

On occasion you may find a day when special cleaning and organizing feels just right. With a giant sorting mat, children can collect, count, and organize materials on "Inventory Day."

1. Using brightly colored electrical tape, divide a plastic tablecloth into sections to create a large sorting mat.

2. Place one item in each section to create sorting "labels." For example, place a mixing spoon at the top of one section to indicate to children that all the mixing spoons belong in that section. Do the same with other categories of items.

3. Give each child a dishpan (or other container) in which to place ten items for sorting. Have children bring the items to the sorting mat and sort them. They can then return for more items to sort. Repeat this procedure until all items have been sorted.

4. To go further with the sorting, use sentence strips to label each sorting mat section.

5. Guide children in counting the items in each section, and in completing an inventory form. (See reproducible Inventory Day Record Sheet, page 24.)

6. Have children replace the items in each section in an orderly way, eliminating those that are broken, have parts missing, or just don't belong. Admire children's organizing efforts!

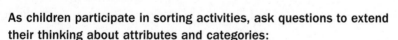

" Math Talk "

As children participate in sorting activities, ask questions to extend their thinking about attributes and categories:

- I wonder where this one goes. What do you think?
- What is another way to sort everything in this group?
- How are these the same? How are they different?
- I wonder: Why doesn't this one work here?

Teaching Tip

Have children begin with sorting into categories, then go further by having them sort the items into subcategories (which also promotes understanding of inclusive and exclusive sets). For example, children can further sort spoons by attributes such as size (big spoons, medium spoons, small spoons) or material (wooden, plastic, metal). As children increase the number of attributes they use in their sorting (it's a spoon and it's big), they refine their understanding of categories.

66 Math Talk 99

Talk About Sorting

From organizing dishes at the dramatic play center to sorting books on shelves, a classroom is full of opportunities to build math skills related to sorting objects and comparing groups. The following questions are starting points for conversations that might occur before, during, or after sorting activities:

- What is something you notice about these objects? How are some of them alike?
- What are some ways to organize these objects into two groups (three, four, and so on)?
- What can you tell me about the way you sorted these objects?
- I wonder where this one would go. What do you think?
- How are these alike? How are they different?
- I wonder why this one doesn't belong here. What do you think?
- Could any of these go in every group? Why do you think so?
- I can see that the objects in this group are all the same shape (size, color). How do you think you could further sort these objects? (For example, a child might sort utensils at the dramatic play area by type—spoons, forks, and chopsticks. The child might then further sort the spoons by material—plastic, metal, wood.)

66 Math Talk 99

Talk About Shapes

As young children explore shapes around the room (such as with blocks or in an art project), use questions such as those that follow to encourage understanding of the properties of shapes and recognition of their names. Children's understanding will grow throughout the grades with experiences that revisit and expand on related concepts and skills.

- Do you know the name for the shape you are using? What do you know about this shape that can help you find another just like it?
- I notice you're using a lot of rectangles in your project (picture, block tower). Where else are these shapes important? *(Notice shapes in the room.)*
- What happens when we turn this shape like this? *(Turn shape for different perspective.)* Is it still the same shape? How do you know?
- This shape has [*Describe a feature of shape, such as "four sides"*]. Do you see objects around the room that have this shape? How are they alike?

Integrating Math Into the Early Childhood Classroom Scholastic Teaching Resources

" Math Talk "

Talk About Number Lines

Number lines are a source of great interest for young children. Each time children visit a number line in the classroom is an opportunity for making mathematical connections. As children explore number lines, ask questions that reinforce what they know about numbers, and then take that knowledge a little further.

- Some numbers have straight lines. Where do you see numbers with straight lines? Do you know the names for these numbers?

- Some numbers have curved lines. Where do you see numbers with curved lines? Do you know the names for these numbers?

- I see a number that tells how old you are. Can you find it? What number comes just before? Just after?

- How are these numbers (1–9) alike?

- How are these numbers (9 and 10) different?

- Where else do you see numbers in the classroom? What do those numbers tell you? (For example, numbers on a clock tell the time; numbers on a calendar tell the date; numbers in books tell the page; numbers on the classroom door tell the classroom.)

" Math Talk "

Talk About Graphs

Graph displays are a continual source of opportunities for encouraging use of math language. Adapt the following questions to use with graphs:

- What question does our graph help to answer?

- Are there more _____ or _____ ? (For example, Are there more children with birthdays in October or March?)

- Are there fewer _____ or _____ ? (For example, Are there fewer jars of red paint or blue paint?)

- How many more _____ than _____ ? (For example, How many more sunny days than rainy days were there this week?)

- Are there as many _____ as _____ ? How do you know? (For example, Are there as many juice boxes for snack as there are water bottles?)

- How many fewer _____ than _____ ? (For example, How many fewer children prefer vanilla ice cream than chocolate ice cream?)

- What is surprising about the information on our graph?

Name _____ Date _____

Inventory Day Record Sheet

We sorted the kitchen supplies. Then we counted them.

Here's what we found out! We have:

_____ Bowls

_____ Plates

_____ Cups

_____ Forks

_____ Spoons

_____ Knives

_____ Bread

_____ Cans of Food

_____ Fruits and Vegetables

_____ Meat and Fish

_____ Milk and Juice

_____ Pots and Pans

_____ Other

Integrating Math Into the Early Childhood Classroom Scholastic Teaching Resources

Rituals and Routines

Standards Connections					
Activity	Number and Operations	Algebra	Geometry	Measurement	Data Analysis
Chants and Patterns	•	•	•		•
Presenting the Count and Countess!	•	•	•		•
Morning Meeting Survey Plates	•	•			•
Calendar Connections	•	•		•	•
Calendar Count-Up/ Countdown	•	•		•	
Double-Chain Discoveries	•	•	•	•	•
From One to Five	•	•			
Snack Table Centerpieces	•	•			•
Tickets, Please	•		•		•
Napkins and Numbers	•	•	•		
Snack Mat Math	•	•	•	•	•
Raisin Box Investigations	•		•	•	•
I Spy Snacks		•	•		
The Snack Count and Countess	•				
Cookie Count	•	•			
Do We Have Enough?	•	•		•	
Snack Graphs	•	•		•	•

Teaching Tip

Teacher-directed instruction is but one means by which children acquire understanding. Care should be taken that active, hands-on learning is a cornerstone of curriculum planning. With this in mind, play is as important in a half-day as in a full-day kindergarten so that children can construct meaningful connections.

Attendance, Morning Meeting, calendar time, and transitions are just a few of the common rituals and routines experienced by most children in early childhood settings. There are opportunities to infuse each of these common times of the day with math-rich connections. The challenge is to look at the predictable, daily activities and to ask ourselves if we might offer richer learning by revising our preconceived ideas about routine times of the day. Among the activities in this section, attendance takes a rhythmic twist with a lively chant that connects counting, line-up becomes a number-identification opportunity, calendar time serves as a platform for exploring number groupings, and snack time inspires rich math conversations.

Chants and Patterns

Young children enjoy the natural rhythms and repetitions of chants. Using chants in the classroom offers children opportunities to notice the relationships that create patterns. Use the following chants to welcome children to school and to support smooth transitions from one activity to the next.

Who's Here?

This chant lets children rhyme and count their way through the morning attendance. Use it in conjunction with the attendance board or graph (see page 16) to enliven this daily routine. As children clap or tap out the sound in each child's name, they'll also do some auditory matching to tie literacy and math together.

"Selective exposure to and experiences with music feeds children's developing mathematical concepts and skills of classification, comparison, ordering, measuring, and graphing."

(Shilling, 2002)

Who's here?

Say it clear

So we hear which friends are near...

So-phie, Jes-si-ca, Jon, An-drew, Al-ex-an-der . . .

1. Have children gather together in a circle (as for Morning Meeting). As you recite the chant together, pass a rhythm stick around the circle as they each take a turn tapping and sounding out their name.

2. To extend the activity, let children sort themselves into groups by the number of syllables in their names.

3. For independent practice, stock a sorting station with name/picture cards of children in the class. Children can repeat the activity, sorting the cards into groups by the number of syllables they hear in each name.

Clap, Clap, Tap, Tap

This lively chant invites children to listen to and join in on patterns they hear.

Clap, clap, tap, tap

One, two, three

[Hold up your fingers in turn.]

Now everyone has eyes on me!

[Point to your eyes.]

Clap, clap, tap, tap

[Create a simple clap, tap pattern for the children to follow.]

One, two, three

[Hold up your fingers in turn.]

Listen and then you follow me.

[Repeat the pattern and have children repeat.]

Experiment with using pattern blocks and cubes to represent the patterns children recognize in chants.

1. As you recite line 1 of this chant, change where you are tapping so children really do follow with their eyes.

2. Have children join in by holding up one, two, and then three fingers as you recite lines 2 and 5. They can point to their eyes as they follow along with line 3.

3. Once children are familiar with the chant, invite them to join in on clapping and tapping. Then let them take turns creating patterns for the class to repeat.

Missing Number Chant

This chant invites children to chime in to practice the numerals 1–5 (or 1–10 if you choose).

Hi-Ho the Derry-o

A number is missing

Where did it go?

Sort out the numbers

And you will see

Which number it could be!

Numeral Cards

| 1 | 2 | 3 | 4 | 5 |
| 6 | 7 | 8 | 9 | 10 |

1. Copy the Numeral Cards reproducible (page 37) and cut the cards apart. Set aside any numerals you do not wish to use. Provide a number line as reference to help children organize the numerals in order as they play.

2. Remove one card from the set and place it in an envelope. Place the remaining cards in a fancy Number Box, decorated to look like a treasure box.

continued

3. Have children gather together in a seated circle. Give the envelope to one child. Then shake the box as you recite the chant.

4. Invite a child to open the box and place the cards faceup for all to see. Let this child determine which card is missing, with a little help from a classmate (or you) if necessary.

5. The child holding the envelope checks to see if the missing number is in the envelope. This child becomes the next one to guess the missing number.

Presenting the Count and Countess!

Outfitted in a royal cape with counting wand in hand, the class Count or Countess is ready to report on such math-related routines as attendance and weather. Rotate the honor to make sure each child has a chance to play the part. Use the related record sheet (page 38) to summarize the counting news that the children report. They can then share their experience as Count or Countess at home. Following is a sampling of duties suitable for a young Count or Countess:

1. Use the attendance board or graph (see page 16) to count the number of children absent or present.

2. Count the number of children at the Morning Meeting, using the wand to gently touch each in turn on the shoulder (or tap in front of them); classmates can join in on the counting as they are comfortable.

3. Announce the date, then lead the class in clapping and counting up to that number.

4. Report on the weather of the day and share graph results showing weather over time—for example, "There have been two more sunny days than cloudy days this month."

5. Discuss results of informal surveys using data from class graphs, asking, for example, "Do more of us prefer vanilla or chocolate ice cream?"

" Math Talk "

Notice opportunities within the Count's or Countess's daily reports to ask questions that invite the use of mathematical thinking and language—for example:

- How does the number of students here today compare with the number here yesterday?

- What do you notice about today's date? (for example, "It's a two-digit number" or "It's the same number as the one that tells how old I am!")

- Has this week been mostly sunny or mostly cloudy? How can you tell?

A counting wand is very much like a pointer for reading. To make one, cover a gift-wrap tube (or mailing cylinder, which is sturdier) with colorful paper or contact paper and attach ribbons to one end. A colorful crown and cape will complete the costume for the day's Count or Countess.

Morning Meeting Survey Plates

The Morning Meeting is an excellent time to take a survey. Children are gathered together and can use results of the survey to get to know their classmates better. Paper or polystyrene plates make excellent vehicles for data collection on any number of topics.

1. Write each child's name on a spring-type clothespin. Use permanent or paint markers. Have children select their clothespins before sitting in a circle.

2. To begin with some simple Yes/No surveys, write "Yes" on one plate and "No" on a second plate.

3. Share a "Yes" or "No" data-collection question—for example, "Did you play outside during that snowstorm yesterday?"

4. Pass the plates around the circle. Invite children to register their responses by clipping their clothespin to the appropriate plate.

5. When the plates have made their way around the circle, count the clothespins on each plate and discuss results.

6. As a variation, use the plates to vote on choices—for example, "Let's find out if our class wants to turn the house area into a doctor's office or a pet shop" or "Do you want to read about dinosaurs or dragons today?" Place a picture on each plate to help children determine which plate gets their clothespin vote.

Calendar Connections

Traditionally, a substantial amount of time during the Morning Meeting is spent on the calendar. The rich learning is not in the calendar itself, but rather in the pattern and progression of numbers up to a point and then repeating this for the next month.

March						
Sunday	Monday	Tuesday	Wednesday	Thursday	Friday	Saturday
						1
2	3	4	5	6	7	8
9	10	11	12	13	14	15
16	17	18	19	20	21	22
23	24	25	26	27	28	29
30	31					

Keep in mind that young children do not easily understand the numbers at the upper end of the month (28–31). A vertical number line is a more helpful math connection for four- and five-year-olds. Display a vertical number line up to 31 alongside the traditional calendar. Use the number line to let children count up to the last number of the month. Guide children to notice place value changes in the number line—for example, after 9, 19, and 29. (Notice the change to 10, 20, and 30.)

Teaching Tip

The paper-plate method of data collection works well for the daily lunch count, too. (See Lunch Count, page 18.)

During group
meeting time,
model how to use
math materials to
prepare students for
independent activities
during choice time.

Calendar Count-Up

Choose a special occasion children can look forward to—such as the first day of spring, the one hundredth day of school, or the beginning of a school vacation—and create a colorful paper chain to count up to the big day!

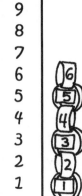

1. Count on a calendar to determine the number of days until the special occasion. Make the same number of paper-chain links and place them in a basket or bag. (Size paper chain links so that they will align with numbers on a vertical number line.) Display a vertical number line to give children a reference to the progression of days. (The number line goes from 1 up to the number of days until the special occasion.)

2. Each day, have the Count or Countess (see page 28) add a link to the chain (display next to the number line). Write the corresponding numeral on each link. (Use small sticky notes so all numerals are facing front. See illustration, right.) Mark off the tens with special colors or decorations.

3. Use the number line to make a connection to the number of days that have gone by and the number of days that remain. (Say, for example: *Eight days have gone by. Only two more days before we go apple picking!*) This exercise, repeated daily, helps children develop a "mental" number line and begin to develop an understanding of number relationships. They learn, for example, which numbers are next to each other (when they see an 8, they know there's a 9 on one side and a 7 on the other), and how many numbers are between other numbers—for example, between 5 and 9. After repeated experience, use more challenging numbers, such as 11 and 14. When you get to the magic number, it is time to celebrate!

Use the calendar count-up and countdown (see page 31) to encourage development of math vocabulary related to time and measurement.

- How many days have gone by since we began our count?

- Do we have as many (more, fewer) days to go until our special day? How can you tell?

- Are we past the middle mark? How can you use the number line to tell?

- If today we have ten days to go until our special event, how many did we have yesterday? How many will we have tomorrow?

Calendar Countdown

As a variation to counting up to special days, use paper-chain links to count down to a special day.

1. Count with children the number of days in a new month, and the number of days until a special event. Then introduce the corresponding numeral.

2. Have children work together to make a paper chain with the same number of links as number of days in the new month. Use links in special colors to mark significant days (such as orange for Halloween). Also mark the special days on a traditional calendar. Display the paper chain next to a vertical number line to support children in understanding the progression of days.

3. Each day, have the Count or Countess (see page 28) remove a link from the paper chain and announce the number of days remaining until the special day arrives.

Double-Chain Discoveries

To take math concepts further, let children experiment with using two chains— one showing the number of days until a special day and one showing the number of days that have elapsed.

1. When removing the first link in a calendar countdown, begin another chain (in a different color) for a calendar count-up. Place the two chains side by side. (Provide a vertical number line as well to encourage connections to number relationships.)

2. As children remove a link from the countdown chain each day to show how many days remain until the special day, have them move the link to the other chain to show how many days have passed since the beginning of the count. Added together, these numbers will equal the target number of days children started with (conservation of number).

From One to Five

Transition times present the perfect opportunity to work on subitizing skills (see Teaching Tip, right). Practice with subitizing one to six objects is sufficient for children in preK–K.

1. Make multiple copies of the counting cards (page 39), enough so each child can have one card. These are simply cards with a number of oversize dots on them. Enlarge the cards if desired.

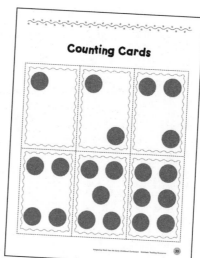

continued

Subitizing refers to the ability to recognize the number of objects in a set without actually counting each individual object. This is an important skill that relates to children's developing number sense. Children who can identify small quantities in arrangements such as those on dominoes or dice, without actually counting them one by one, have a strong sense of quantity.

2. Distribute a card to each student. To transition to the next activity, call students by a number—for example, *Anyone with a three-dot card can go and wash up for snack.* Or use the cards to play a movement game. Hold up a card and say, *Anyone with this number of dots can jump four times.*

3. Use the cards for repeated practice to develop students' ability to recognize (how many) without counting.

Snack Table Centerpieces

Incorporate snack-time centerpieces that reinforce number recognition.

1. Create a centerpiece for each table that visually represents the table number (arbitrary numbers are fine; it is not necessary that they are in sequence). For example, place the number of flowers (in a vase) at each table that corresponds to the table's number (five flowers at table 5, three flowers at table 3, and so on). Other centerpiece options include buttons on polystyrene snowmen and groupings of toy animals. Change the table numbers regularly to provide new counting and number-recognition experiences.

2. Incorporate a sign with the table number written on it into the centerpieces.

3. During snack time, notice with children whether the tables have the same number of people. If some tables have more or fewer, invite children to determine how many more or fewer (and notice how they do this).

Teaching Tip

Snack time is a relaxing time in the day when teachers and children sit down together to share news of their lives and enjoy one another's company. There are many ways to casually weave math into conversation. There are also special activities to enrich snack time. However, teaching is not the primary function of snack time. It should be kept as an "extra," after sharing and conversation has been given a fair amount of focus.

Tickets, Please

Tickets to snack time provide children with practice at recognizing the number of objects in a group with and without counting and help them develop an understanding of "how many."

1. On tagboard "tickets," make a set of dots (or any other shape) that correspond to table numbers. (Make as many tickets for each table as there are seats.)

2. As children prepare to transition to snack time, give each one a ticket. Children match the number of dots on their ticket to the table number, then take a seat. (As a variation, you may also have children match numerals on their tickets to those at the tables.)

Math Talk

Using snack time as a springboard for math discussions, invite further exploration:

- How many shoes are under table 2? How might we figure that out?
- Are there more shoes at table 2 or table 4? How can you find out?
- If everyone at table 4 and table 2 switched seats, which table would I find the most shoes under? How do you know?

Repeat similar questions to include each table. Note that Unifix cubes or links work well for this kind of problem solving.

Napkins and Numbers

Small napkins are a nice addition to the snack table, especially with colorful numerals stamped on them.

1. Using nontoxic ink, stamp a numeral on each napkin. You might also stamp the corresponding number of dots or shapes on the napkins to reinforce counting skills.

2. During snack time, invite everyone to notice their napkin: *How many 1s at your table? Which table has more 5s than 3s?* Invite children to wave their napkins in numerical order: *Is any number missing at a table? What is it?*

Teaching Tip

Children can use a damp cloth to clean their laminated place mats. For sanitary purposes, follow up (teacher-use only) with a bleach solution of ¼ teaspoon bleach to 1 quart water. (Use permanent marker to label the container with its contents; keep out of children's reach.)

Snack Mat Math

These place mats are easy to make and fun to use during snack time and invite spontaneous math-related explorations, including those related to counting, one-to-one correspondence, constructing and deconstructing numbers, measurement, and geometry.

Use the illustrations that follow as models for making snack mats. Decorate the place mat edges if desired. Laminate the mats for cleanliness and durability (or cover with clear contact paper). Model various ways of using the snack mats before having children choose their own to use. Suggestions follow.

Ten-Frame Snack Mat: Count up as you place a fish cracker in each section of a ten frame (see page 40). Count backward as you eat each one. Along the way, relate the number ten to the number of boxes that are empty and that still have crackers on them—for example, *The number ten is made up of four empty boxes and six boxes that still have crackers on them.*

Shape Snack Mats: Shape mats offer an opportunity to start a conversation with, *I'm thinking of a snack that has a triangle shape.* Have children hunt for the snack that fits the description. Together, use the snacks to notice that triangles, for example, can come in different sizes and shapes.

Measuring Snack Mats: Lines of various lengths on the mats can be used to measure the length of snacks. Ask: *Is that line longer or shorter than your string cheese?*

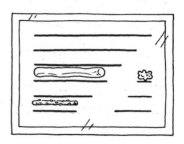

Checkerboard Snack Mat: A checkerboard design on mats allows children a chance to develop one-to-one correspondence as they place raisins, popcorn, or goldfish in each box. They can use the same mat to create patterns.

Graphing Snack Mats: Use a mat with a graphing template to find out how many of each color are in a handful of fruity cereal Os. Ask: *How many red pieces? Green? Yellow? Blue? Orange?* Or graph gummy fruits to find out how many of each shape are in a snack pack.

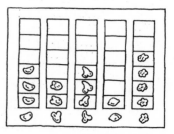

Raisin Box Investigations

Snack-size boxes of raisins seem to be made for math investigations. Give each child a snack-size box of raisins and use these ideas to get started:

- Let children have fun guessing how many raisins are inside. Then have them use a ten-frame mat, placing their raisins one to a section. Once the ten sections are filled, have children place those ten raisins to the side, and count out ten more (again placing raisins one to a section). Continue until children cannot fill their ten frame with the raisins that remain. These are the "extras." Children now count the raisins by tens, and count on by ones with the extras. Have children compare the number of raisins. Ask: *Are there the same number of raisins in every snack-size box? If not, what's the greatest number of raisins? Least?*

- Using a shape mat, have children guess how many raisins will fit end to end around the perimeter of one of the shapes. Ask: *Will more raisins fit around a triangle or a square? A rectangle or a circle?* Let them discuss and test their ideas. Then they can eat this math exploration!

I Spy Snacks

Play an attribute game at the snack table to build math vocabulary, reinforce knowledge of shapes, and more. Simply describe a snack you see by attributes—for example:

I spy a snack that is red.

I spy a snack that is round.

I spy a snack that is long and skinny.

Have children listen and look to decide if the snack you describe belongs to them. Children can take turns describing attributes, too.

"Math Talk"

Use prompts such as these to spark math-rich conversations at snack time:

- If you eat one, how many do you think will be left?
- How many will you have left if you eat two more?
- I wonder: How many carrot sticks will equal the length of this line?
- Are there enough raisins in your box to fill each square? What part of the checkerboard do you think they'll fill?

Teaching Tip

For quick and easy snacks children can make and enjoy, see the Cooking Activities section, page 99.

The Snack Count and Countess

Let children at each table roll a die to see who will be the Snack Count or Countess that day. The person who rolls the highest/lowest number can be the Count or Countess. The Count or Countess chooses something to count at the table, such as the number of people with juice boxes or the number of people with a snack that is red. The Count/Countess can bring home the Count/Countess record sheet (page 38) with the day's data on it.

Cookie Count

Read *The Doorbell Rang* by Pat Hutchins (Greenwillow, 1986) during story time. Then follow up at snack time with a playful, story-based chant that incorporates math concepts.

1. Display a plate of plastic cookies (or those made from play clay). Recite the following chant, filling in a number that is equal to or less than the number of cookies on the plate:

   Cookies, cookies at the door
   If I ate___, could you eat any more?

2. Have children figure out if there are any cookies left for them, and if so, how many. Change the number in the chant each time.

Do We Have Enough?

This is a good activity for days when you have a helper. It can be used with snacks such as popcorn, raisins, and apple slices.

1. Place a plate of snacks at each table.

2. Have children take turns estimating whether or not each child at the table will be able to have one, two, or three (or more).

3. Have children develop and test a process for finding out the answer. Then they can share the snacks equally.

Snack Graphs

The end of snack time is not just for cleanup. Take a few minutes for some graphing fun.

1. Have children place the roll-out graphs (see page 19) on the floor and weight the corners with blocks (or use sticky tack).

2. Graph drink containers by type or contents—for example, juice box/drink pouch/milk carton/thermos/cup or soy milk/cow's milk/juice/water.

3. Graph any snack packaging by type—for example, fruit roll-up wrappers, cheese stick wrappers, cracker bags, and yogurt cups.

Numeral Cards

5	10
4	6_
3	8
2	7
1	9_

Integrating Math Into the Early Childhood Classroom Scholastic Teaching Resources

News From Count _____ **Date** _____

I counted a lot today

And I had a lot to say.

Here is my big counting news

Because numbers are such fun to use!

_____

_____

_____

News From Countess _____ **Date** _____

I counted a lot today

And I had a lot to say.

Here is my big counting news

Because numbers are such fun to use!

_____

_____

_____

Integrating Math Into the Early Childhood Classroom   Scholastic Teaching Resources

Counting Cards

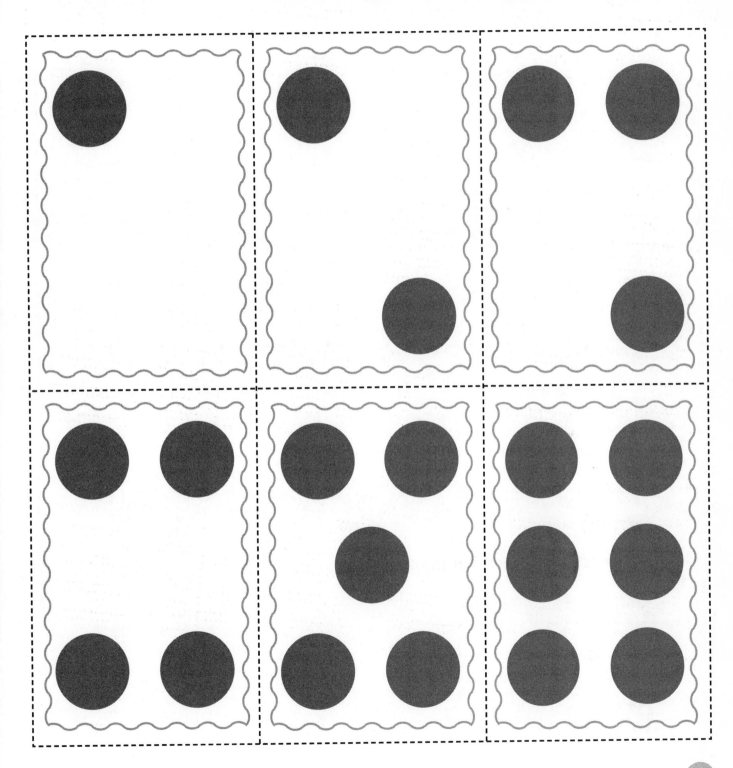

Integrating Math Into the Early Childhood Classroom Scholastic Teaching Resources

Ten Frame

Integrating Math Into the Early Childhood Classroom Scholastic Teaching Resources

Sensory Explorations

Standards Connections

Activity	Number and Operations	Algebra	Geometry	Measurement	Data Analysis
Fast or Slow? (Sensory Table)	•	•		•	
Halfway (Sensory Table)	•	•	•	•	
Snow Much Fun (Sensory Table)	•		•	•	•
Ice Age (Sensory Table)		•	•	•	•
Air Power (Sensory Table)	•	•			•
Treasure Hunt	•		•		
Sort Boards	•	•	•	•	•
Ten Little Piggies	•	•	•	•	•
Shake It Up Seriation: Can Your Ears Tell?	•				
Auditory Patterns	•	•			
Clap It Up!	•	•			
Trace-and-Touch Numerals	•		•		
Shaving Cream Numerals	•		•		
Number Rubbings	•		•		
Blowing Bubbles	•	•	•		
Make Play Clay	•	•	•	•	
Muffin-Tin Problems	•	•	•	•	
Decorating Cookies					
Hunt for Ten	•	•	•		•
Snipping Hot Dogs	•	•	•	•	•

The sensory area allows children an opportunity to feel materials—feel how big, how long, how heavy, or how small something is. As they interact with materials, children construct understandings related to the attributes associated with objects. Children learn quickly how heavy a block is by carrying it. They learn "how long" by stretching a string from one end of a object to the other end. Children love to feel attributes, as well, and the sensory area is the place to make that happen. It is delightful to watch children at play in sand and water. They make roads and mountains. They fill bottles and empty them, then scoop them full again and repeat over and over. They identify tools they want to use and trade containers when another size feels more appropriate.

A rich assortment of materials invites active learning and challenges children to extend their thinking, engage in problem solving, and express themselves in specific language. The bigger bucket, the larger scoop, the highest mountain, and the deepest ocean are all specific terms children use naturally in the sensory area.

Organizing the Sensory Area

This section of the room, as all others, needs to be carefully organized, with many sizes of containers, scoopers, funnels, boats, cars, tubes, droppers, and water/sand wheels all within sight and easy reach.

- Store utensils, containers, and other materials in plastic bins labeled with words and pictures. Add numerals to tell children how many cars, boats, or spoons they will find in a bucket. (This also helps them when it's time to clean up.)

- Stock the sensory area with paper, crayons, pencils, and markers to encourage children to record their discoveries or data associated with their investigations. These records become tangible documents of the rich learning that takes place in the sensory area.

- Rotate new materials into the sensory area throughout the year. Children become accustomed to some kinds of things and may lose interest. A new set of sand or water toys brings back the novelty and the interest and encourages fresh approaches to problem solving and learning.

Fast or Slow? (Sensory Table)

Gather a number of disposable plastic drinking cups and poke a variety of holes in the bottoms of them. Some should have many small holes, others should have medium-size holes, and still others should have a single large hole. Have children compare and contrast the speed with which water "disappears" or leaks out of the cups.

Halfway (Sensory Table)

Place a number of containers of various sizes in the sensory table. Mark the halfway spot with a line on the container. Ask: *How many scoops of water (or sand or another sensory table filler) does it take to fill a container halfway? How many scoops will it take to fill it all the way?*

Math Talk

It's important to plan time to interact with children as they explore at the sand and water table. Talking at the sensory table offers children a chance to use mathematical language and to experiment with size, weight, and capacity.

- How many scoops does it take to fill up this container? How many to fill it halfway?
- How many scoops will it take to fill the container using this cup compared with using this other cup?
- How many more scoops do you think it will take to fill your bucket?
- Your container looks bigger than mine. How could we find out which one holds more water?

Snow Much Fun (Sensory Table)

Fill a sensory (water) table with snow. Let children play with the snow using droppers and food coloring. Then invite them to investigate how fast snow melts. But start a timer first!

1. Every five minutes, check in with children for a report on the speed of the melting: *Has a lot melted? Has half melted?*

2. When all the snow has melted, invite children to guess how many cups of water are in the water table, then measure and count.

3. With children, document one melting experience, then compare the results with a new melting experience.

As an extension, provide a sand timer or digital timer. Children can add to their discoveries by timing how long it takes for different containers to drain.

Ice Age (Sensory Table)

Ice—and melting ice—provide for extended observation and discovery related to concepts of time and measurement.

1. Place several buckets of ice cubes in the water table. Notice how high the ice cubes reach. (You may mark it with waterproof tape.)

2. Then notice the height of the water as the ice cubes melt. You might try timing the melting by placing a clock nearby. Talk with children about how long they think it will take the ice to melt. Incorporate concepts of a "long time" (for example, until lunch) or a "short time" (until snack) to assist children in constructing knowledge relating to segments of time.

3. As a variation, fill the water table with ice just covering the bottom. Mark the height of the ice with a piece of waterproof tape. Place a timer by the water table and have children set it for 15-minute intervals. How many minutes will it take for all the ice to melt? What is the height of the water compared with the original height of the ice?

Math Talk

Guide children in making math connections beginning with how high the snow or ice is in the water table when they start. Comparisons will come naturally as they observe the snow melting.

- How high is the snow when you start?
- How high is the water after the snow melts?
- How long did it take the snow to melt?
- Did the snow take up the same amount of space as the water does now? Why do you think this is so?

Air Power (Sensory Table)

Plastic boats are fun to move about a water table, and they invite explorations that connect number, time, distance, and speed.

1. Fill a water table with water and float some small plastic boats in it. Give each child at the table a straw.

2. Let children experiment to find out how many puffs it takes to move a boat from

one end of the table to the other, then from one side to the other. Children can work in pairs, with one counting while the other blows through the straw to move the boat. Provide a clipboard, paper, and pencil for children to experiment with making tallies.

Treasure Hunt (Sensory Table)

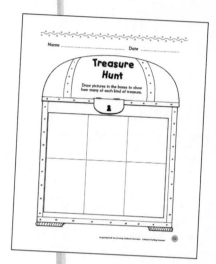

A treasure hunt at the sand table is full of suspense and excitement—and opportunities for children to count, keep tallies, explore attributes, and more.

1. In the sand table, bury items associated with a theme or unit—for example, plastic dinosaurs (for a dinosaur unit), toy cars (for a transportation theme), jewels and "gold" coins (for a castle theme), or plastic bugs (for a spring or insects unit).

2. Let children hunt for the buried treasure and document their findings on the record sheet provided (page 51) or by drawing pictures of their treasures on a sheet of paper.

 Math Talk

Children can use their record sheets as a guide to discuss their discoveries at circle time, snack time, or a closing time at the end of the day. This way they can both represent and articulate their findings. As time allows, you might record children's comments on their record sheets to serve as further documentation of their learning. Questions to spark conversations include:

- How are Ann's and William's discoveries alike? How are they different?
- I noticed there were some red jewels in the sand table today. Did anyone find jewels that could go in a collection of red jewels? What other collections of jewels could we have?
- Some of you found coins today. What did you notice about those coins? (Incorporate discussion of size, shape, numbers, and so on.)

Sort Boards

Fill the table with different types of small items (in a variety of sizes and colors), such as buttons or dried beans to inspire explorations that involve counting and sorting and measuring time.

1. Provide children with sort boards (page 52). Model how to sort the items by an identifiable attribute, such as type, color, or size. How many of each can children find in a scoop? Have children scoop up the items, and sort them on the sort board. (Children can also sort into small containers.)

continued

The sensory table can become a planting center when spring arrives. Stock the sensory table with potting soil, seeds, small peat pots, scoops, and spoons. Display numbered steps for planting seeds. (See Garden Center, page 82, for more information.)

2. To add a measurement element, provide a timer. How many of a particular type of item can children find in two minutes? Four minutes?

3. As a variation, randomly bury in the sand table items that represent several categories, such as small plastic animals, buttons, or links. Have children find and sort the items by their own sorting rules (such as by color, type, and size).

Ten Little Piggies

The familiar counting rhyme "This Little Piggy" is a childhood staple. Use the rhyme as a springboard for an activity that lets children count toes by tens.

1. Tape several lengths of roll paper to the floor.

2. Paint the bottom of each child's feet (one child at a time). Have the child walk across the paper, making footprints until the paint runs out. Label each child's footprints.

3. When the paint is dry, count the number of footprints each child made.

4. Cut out each child's strip of footprints. Count by tens to see how many "piggies" in each child's strip of footprints and how many piggies total for the class.

Shake It Up Seriation: Can Your Ears Tell?

Dried beans in canisters make instant shakers and invite children to wonder: How many beans do I hear in there?

1. Place different numbers of dried beans in film canisters—very few (even just one) in some, and more in others.

2. Let children shake the canisters and listen to figure out which one has the fewest beans and which has the most.

3. Have children order the canisters by amount, from least to most. They can open the canisters, pour out the contents, and count to see how they did.

Auditory Patterns

Clap a pattern and have children repeat it. Clap again and ask children to count the number of claps. Then repeat with them and count together. When children get skilled at this, add tapping to the auditory patterns. Repeat and offer support as needed to help children develop strategies for counting the sounds they hear.

Clap It Up!

While children wait for their turn during any transition (such as small groups washing up for lunch), this listening/counting activity will require good concentration. Have children close their eyes and listen and count as you clap two to ten times. Children repeat what they have heard, and then report that number.

Trace-and-Touch Numerals

Tracing large, textured numerals helps children form number shapes on their own.

1. On large oaktag squares, write numerals (one per square). Make multiple sets of numerals with different textures. Let children use small glue bottles to fill in each numeral.

2. While the glue is still wet, have children sprinkle the numerals with colored sand, glitter, cotton balls, or small dried pasta shapes (consider coloring the dried pasta with liquid watercolor first).

3. When the glue has dried, children can trace the numerals with their fingers. They can say the names for numbers they know, place the cards in numerical order, group them in same-number sets (all 3s, all 4s, and so on), and try forming the same numerals on their own.

4. Guide children to notice that though the feel may change, the quantity that a numeral represents is always the same.

 Math Talk

Use the textured numeral cards to explore numeral shapes and recognition.

- Which numerals have only straight lines? Only curved lines? Both straight and curved lines. [*Have children trace straight and curved lines in the air.*] What are some other ways we could sort these numerals?

- [*Hold up two numeral cards.*] How are these number shapes alike? How are they different?

- Do you have a favorite number? Can you find it here? What kind of lines (curved, straight) do you see in your favorite number?

Shaving Cream Numerals

Children are naturally drawn to this delightful sensory experience. Just squirt a little shaving cream at each child's place. Children can practice numeral writing (but only after there has been time to enjoy the feel of the shaving cream itself!).

Number Rubbings

Feel those numbers! Children can do rubbings of numerals cut from sandpaper (glue sandpaper to tagboard before cutting out numerals) or corrugated cardboard. Children can make a rubbing by simply placing paper over the textured numerals and coloring with crayon or pencil over the shape. For fun, children can select a numeral without looking and try to identify it as they make the rubbing. Ask: *Can you feel the numeral you are rubbing? Do you feel straight lines? Curved lines? What can you tell about this numeral from its shape?*

Blowing Bubbles

Bubble blowing is a good warm-weather activity and invites development of descriptive language for size comparisons and positions, such as *big*, *small*, *tiny*, *many*, *high*, and *low*. Labeled photographs of children blowing bubbles make a good class book to support this vocabulary development.

Make Play Clay

A fresh batch of play clay is always a treat. As you mix up the dough, children can help identify numerals in the recipe, give directions in order, scoop (and count) ingredients, and so on. Here's a favorite recipe:

3 cups water	3 tablespoons cream of tartar
3 cups flour	1½ cups salt
3 tablespoons vegetable oil	food coloring (optional)

1. Mix water, flour, oil, cream of tartar, and salt in a saucepan. Stir over medium heat (adult only) until ingredients are thoroughly combined (about 15 minutes).

2. When cool, add food coloring (if desired) and knead the dough until color is evenly absorbed.

3. Store play clay in a sealed container when not in use.

Muffin-Tin Problems

Will a ball of play clay be enough to fill the muffin tin? Young bakers will enjoy baking up some "muffins" to see what they learn.

1. Let children estimate how many muffins they can make with the clay. Ask: *Do you have enough to fill the tin? Will you have some left over? How much?*

2. Once the muffins have been made, see what else children can do with the clay. Ask: *If they roll it, will it be long enough to reach from one side of a snack mat to the other? Will it stretch to reach across the table?* Try it and find out.

" Math Talk "

Play clay invites endless exploration, much of it filled with math connections. Share these questions to prompt conversations about measurement.

- About how much clay do you think you will need to make a cookie for each classmate? What are some ways to figure that out?

- That lump of clay is big! Do you think if you roll it and stretch it out it will be as long as this string? How can we find out?

Decorating Cookies

Add large sequins to the play-clay table for a cookie-decorating day—and encourage number-recognition and counting skills in the process.

1. Share a cookie rhyme children can recite as they work in their play clay "bakery."

Cookies

Cookies are good from the bakery shop.
They look so pretty,
You will want to stop
And pick out some cookies and have a treat.
Then share the cookies with the friends you meet.

2. Add an assortment of cookie cutters to the play-clay table, along with a container of large sequins.

continued

3. After children have cut out their cookies, have them select a number card or roll a die to see how many of each sequin they can put on their cookies. Children can count out the corresponding number of sequins and decorate their cookies.

Hunt for Ten

Try hiding ten buttons, beads, or dried beans in the lumps of play clay. As children find them they can put them on a ten-frame mat (see page 40). They will know they have found them all when the mat is full. The use of the ten frame reinforces number concepts and lets children know when the search is over.

Snipping Hot Dogs

Children roll play clay into hot dogs and then divide them to explore concepts of "equal" sharing. This activity is also an engaging way to support the development of fine-motor skills.

1. Invite children to roll play clay into long hot dogs. Ask: *How many pieces can you cut from one long dog?* Have children snip their hot dogs into bite-size pieces. *Will there be enough pieces of hot dog for everyone at the table to have one? How about two?*

2. Recite a poem with children as they explore the idea of sharing those pieces of their hot dogs. Discuss results of their sharing. (See Math Talk, below, for discussion starters.)

Hot Dog

Hot dog grows long and thin.
How many pieces can I cut it in?
Pieces for you, pieces for me,
Pieces for everyone I can see.

Math Talk

Engage children in conversations to explore one-to-one correspondence, equal sets, and measurement.

- That hot dog is long! I wonder if it's as long as this block. What do you think?

- If you eat five bites, will there be five bites left for me, too? How can we find out? Can you show me another way we could share these hot dogs?

- I wonder if your hot dog will fit better in this bun or this bun. [*Show two pieces of paper, each a different size.*] What do you think?

Name _____   Date _____

Treasure Hunt

Draw pictures in the boxes to show how many of each kind of treasure.

Name _____

Date _____

Sort Board

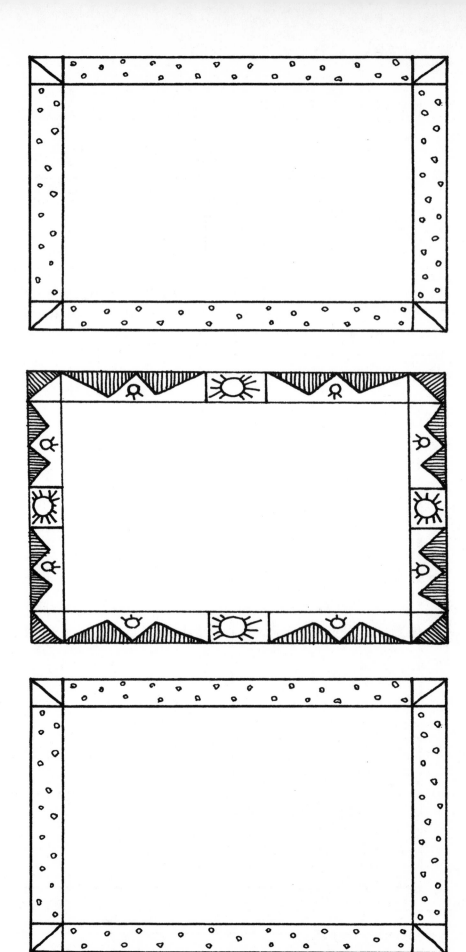

Integrating Math Into the Early Childhood Classroom Scholastic Teaching Resources

Block Center

Standards Connections					
Activity	Number and Operations	Algebra	Geometry	Measurement	Data Analysis
Follow the Leader	●	●	●	●	
Equal-Share Builders	●	●	●		
City Construction Company	●	●	●	●	
The Shape of Signs	●		●		
Bridge It			●	●	
The Block Bank	●	●	●		
Castle Builders	●	●	●	●	
Ramp and Roll		●	●	●	●
Surveyor's Office	●		●	●	
Five-Block Buildings	●	●	●	●	●
Twenty-Block Buildings	●	●	●	●	●
Measure Me	●		●	●	
Who's in the Cave?	●		●	●	
Measuring Kit: Adding Machine Tape and Other Measuring Miracles	●	●	●	●	●
Cleanup Graphs	●	●	●		●

Blocks are a staple of childhood play. Building with blocks engages the imagination, promotes active learning, and stimulates mathematical thinking. As children build trains, towers, even entire cities, they make connections related to number, shape, size (including weight, length, height, depth), patterns, spatial relationships, symmetry, and other key concepts. In order for children to build these understandings, they must explore blocks in an environment rich with learning opportunities. This section offers suggestions for creating such an environment and guiding children in making meaningful mathematical connections.

Organizing the Block Center

Set the stage for learning by providing an organized block center with a wide range of block shapes, sizes, and accessories.

- To facilitate easy sorting and cleanup, label block storage bins or shelves with templates that are exact replicas of the block shapes themselves.

- Include tools for math scaffolding as part of the block corner (see page 54). Index cards, numeral cards, and number stamps are good for giving a building an address (just like real life) and for keeping records of block-building activities. Provide a designated space for paper and clipboards, as well, for creating and recording block stories and architect plans.

- If possible keep a camera in or near the block center. Photos give children a chance to share their building accomplishments in much the same way as their painting.

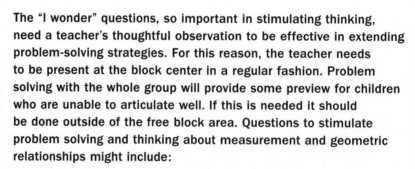

" Math Talk "

The "I wonder" questions, so important in stimulating thinking, need a teacher's thoughtful observation to be effective in extending problem-solving strategies. For this reason, the teacher needs to be present at the block center in a regular fashion. Problem solving with the whole group will provide some preview for children who are unable to articulate well. If this is needed it should be done outside of the free block area. Questions to stimulate problem solving and thinking about measurement and geometric relationships might include:

- I wonder if there are more than ten blocks here. What do you think?
- I wonder: How much taller do you think you can build your tower?
- I wonder: Which blocks are the most important for your building?
- I wonder: Which blocks could you take away without toppling your building?

- Roll-out graphs (see page 19) and sorting boards (see page 52) or hula hoops are particularly helpful at cleanup time. Before they put their blocks away, children can sort them to discover more about the shapes and sizes they used—for example, Which did they use the most of? Fewest of? Did they use the same number of any shapes?

Math-Rich Materials for the Block Center

Stock the block area with materials that will support and inspire mathematical exploration and understanding. Suggestions include:

- Adding machine tape (for measuring)
- Architectural blocks
- Blocks (hollow and solid type; assorted shapes, including ramps)
- Camera
- Castle blocks
- Clipboards
- Clock
- Collections of small figures and objects (toy cars, trucks, emergency vehicles, trains, community helpers and other people, trees, signs, and animals)
- Crayons/pencils/markers
- Dice

- Links (that snap together to make chains, in various colors)
- Numeral cards (page 37)
- Paper
- Ramps and boards
- Roll-out graphs (page 19)
- Solid shapes (triangular and rectangular prisms, cylinders, and cones)
- String/yarn (for measuring)
- Ten frame (page 40)
- Unit blocks (standard sizes: small, medium, and large)
- Unifix cubes
- Windows (play windows from building sets)

Turn windowpane-checked wallpaper or contact paper (as on page 19) into a foundation for buildings that invites children to explore many mathematical ideas—including perimeter and area. Cover posterboard or foam-board rectangles (squares, too) of different sizes with the paper. Model how to use the boards as foundations for buildings. Observe as children use them: How do the varying sizes affect the size of the buildings students construct? Children can explore the differences in the number of "squares" it takes to go around the outside (perimeter) of the building and the number of squares that fill the foundation (area).

Follow the Leader

Children buddy up to play a building game that develops spatial reasoning, builds vocabulary for shapes, and invites exploration of measurement.

1. Gather a set of ten blocks (various shapes and sizes) and spread them out.

2. Have two children work together to match the collection piece by piece to create a matching set of blocks.

3. Introduce the game with a rhyme:

   Leader builds then Follower goes.
   Their building starts and then it grows.
   In the end it looks the same.
   Come and play this building game!

4. Have each child take a set of blocks. One child begins a block structure by selecting and positioning a block. The other child follows, finding a block of the same shape and size, then positioning it in the same way, to start his or her structure. They continue in this way to build duplicate structures.

5. Together, the two children decide which linear part of their structures they would like to measure. Each student then chooses a measuring tool, such as Unifix cubes, adding machine tape, or links, and measures the predetermined part. (They can record their findings on the Block Report, page 66.) They then compare and share their findings with the teacher or classmates. The two can trade places and repeat the activity, so each child has a chance to lead.

Teaching Tip

As a variation, have one student create a structure on one side of a divider. Then remove the divider and have the follower replicate the structure using the second set of matching blocks. Be sure to demonstrate this new approach in a group meeting so there is clear understanding prior to the activity.

" Math Talk "

As children create their block-structure replicas, look for opportunities to draw attention to reasoning and problem-solving skills.

- What is the name for the shape you see? What do you know about this shape that can help you find another just like it?

- Do you think that block is the same size as the one your block buddy used? What are some ways to find out?

- Let's see . . . what block comes next? What do you think?

Equal-Share Builders

Children create and compare sets as they sort blocks to share them equally with partners. Comparing the structures they build helps them develop flexible thinking and vocabulary for shapes and spatial relations.

1. To prepare, combine two matching sets of blocks in one bin. Then share a poem that is just the right length for young builders to learn:

   Big blocks, little blocks, bridge blocks, too,
   Some for me and some for you.
   Equal sharing works just fine.
   Some are yours and some are mine.

2. Have a pair of children sort the blocks so that they have matching sets of blocks.

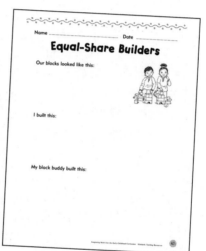

3. Each child builds his or her own building. The two children then compare and contrast their structures. Will they count the same number of blocks in their buildings? Will they find the same shapes? How do they know? They can use the Equal-Share Builders record sheet (page 67) to record what they learn about their structures.

Teaching Tip

Reducing the number of blocks to ten or fewer will better support students in their work on certain assigned activities in the block area.

" Math Talk "

With block-building activities, it is appropriate and engaging to talk with children about not just the height and width of their building but also about its perimeter and area.

- Let's measure the perimeter of your building. That's how long a piece of string is that goes all the way around. Let's estimate how long the string will be. Longer than you are tall? Longer than my desk if we measure around it? About the same length as the number line on the wall?

- Let's investigate the area of your building. That's how many same-size blocks it takes to fill in the outline. How many blocks do you think we will need to fill in this space? What if we use small blocks? What if we use large blocks?

City Construction Company

Transform the block area into a city construction zone that builds math connections in many areas. Children investigate the scale of buildings as they create a skyline—and then use it as a model in their construction projects. They explore concepts of geometry as they investigate the shape of buildings and how they fit into city grids. They develop number concepts as they compare how many blocks it takes to build different structures and how many fit on a city street. All the while, they develop content vocabulary that has a place in the classroom and in everyday life.

1. Share books and photographs about city life. Add them to a display that will inspire and inform children's work as they use blocks to create a city in the classroom.

2. Ask questions to prompt problem solving around city issues—for example: *How do people get around in a city? What kinds of houses are there in a city? What services do people need to live in a city?*

3. Brainstorm characteristics of a city. Make a list with picture cues and add it to the display. This is a good time to introduce "city" vocabulary, such as: *skyscraper, subway, trolley, construction zone,* and *pedestrian.* This special vocabulary complements language for other features of community life, including *grocery store, hospital, school, library, park,* and *fire station.*

4. Have children collaborate on creating a city skyline. Place a large sheet of butcher paper on the floor. (Tape or place blocks on the corners.) Have children use unit blocks to form skyscrapers, placing the base of each building along the bottom of the paper. Some buildings will be high and some will be low. Guide children in tracing the blocks to create an outline of the city. (You might help hold down the blocks as children trace them so the blocks don't move too much.) Children can then add windows, doors, and other features (using collage or drawing). Display at children's eye level in the block area.

Teaching Tip

After laying out the streets, it is crucial that children have some time to work in the area without direction. When they have developed some comfort with this concept, re-tape the area and observe the way in which children approach this now familiar task. To generate further interest and problem-solving opportunities, use blue contact paper to add a river running through the city.

5. Using masking tape, create a street grid on the floor of the block area. Leave plenty of space between city "blocks" to give young children room to maneuver as they build. Watch as children plan and build at this math-rich setup.

6. Here's a rhyme that will keep children thinking as they build structures in their block city.

City Space

City space
Busy place
Roads go here and there.
Buildings high
Buildings low,
So much to see
Everywhere you go!

The Shape of Signs

It is important to help children notice that geometry is everywhere; traffic signs have especially distinctive shapes! Children can make their own traffic signs to add to their city construction.

- Provide stencils for traffic sign shapes. Offer illustrated word cards for reference, so children can use the words as they wish. (Illustrate the signs with appropriate colors so students learn to connect colors, shapes, and words.)

- To further explore shapes, children can experiment with making signs using, for example, only a triangle stencil. This will require some problem solving, and you may be surprised by the results! Two triangles can make a yellow warning sign (such as one that shows a traffic light ahead), or an orange construction sign. Eight triangles can make a stop sign.

- You might print out and post pages from a manual of traffic signs for reference.

Math Talk

Invite children to compare and contrast traffic signs.
Ask questions such as:

- How many sides are there on a stop sign? How many on a yield sign?
- How many more sides does the stop sign have than the yield sign?
- How many different signs are red? What other colors are signs?

To vary children's city construction experiences, tape tagboard squares and rectangles on the floor for building on and around. Use them to inspire problem solving and thoughtful planning. How many same-size blocks does it take to get around a square? How many fit inside? What kinds of buildings can children construct on these bases?

Bridge It

Whether they are crossing a river, connecting two buildings, creating an overpass, or adding a railway, children will have many reasons to build bridges in their block construction projects.

1. To introduce the idea of building bridges, share the classic Norwegian folktale "The Three Billy Goats Gruff." Bright collage illustrations in *The Three Billy Goats Gruff* by Mary Finch (Barefoot Books, 2001) invite young readers to follow along as three billy goats trip-trap over a bridge to enjoy the green grass on the other side.

2. After enjoying the story together, find out what students know about bridges. Pose some questions for them: *How tall could we make a bridge? How long? What would help make a bridge sturdy, so it could hold a truck or train driving across it?*

3. Let children construct block bridges. They can test them out with toy cars, trains, and other vehicles.

The Block Bank

Some children will be builders while others can be bankers! Here's an easy setup for a block "bank" that lets children work with one-to-one correspondence and concepts of money (ones, fives, and tens).

1. Modify egg cartons by removing the end two cups so that only ten sections remain in each carton. (In doing so, you create egg cartons that can double as ten frames.) When children prepare to shop at the "block store," have them take an egg carton and place a penny in each cup (so each child starts with ten pennies).

2. Children then trade pennies for the blocks they wish to buy (one penny per block). They can refill their ten-frame egg carton with pennies as often as they wish.

3. At cleanup time the bankers count all the pennies used to purchase blocks. They can count by ones, or divide pennies into groups of five or ten and skip-count accordingly. Post this number to announce total sales for the day.

Castle Builders

Castles capture a young child's imagination, making them irresistible as block-building projects. Castles also invite problem solving with shapes: What shapes will make walls, towers, turrets, pinnacles, parapets, stairs, doors, and drawbridges? Decorate a crate with pictures of castles and fill it with 20 (or 30) blocks of varying sizes and shapes, then set aside a special area for castle builders to work, and watch as their grand designs take shape!

1. Designate two children each day as the class castle builders. (This helps keep interest high as children look forward to their day as castle builders.)

2. Have children decide among themselves whether the castle will be built vertically for height or horizontally for width. They can decide if there will be rooms and, if so, how many.

3. Children love to learn special vocabulary associated with topics of interest, and that includes castles. As they explore the language of castles, they can decide what special features theirs will have.

4. Let children dictate the story of their castle-building experience. Look for opportunities to infuse their stories with the language of mathematics—for example, help them describe length, height, width, and even perimeter. Photograph children with their castles, and combine the pictures with the stories to make a class Big Book. Children can revisit the book and compare the different structures formed using the same collection of blocks.

5. Children can also use adding machine tape as a measuring tool to document the castle's measurements—using it as a nonstandard measuring tool to find out how high, how wide, how big around, and so on. Label the adding machine tape to provide a record of children's measurements. In this way, children will have a representation of their buildings after they have been dismantled. This also provides a springboard for discussion at home and an affirmation of children's work.

Ramp and Roll

Children can use blocks to build ramps, fun for experimenting with concepts related to the ramp's incline, such as measuring the distance a ball released on the ramp will roll.

1. Invite children to build ramps that vary in length, height, and incline. This will involve some problem solving around how children can increase, for example, the height or incline of a ramp.

2. Provide children with balls of different sizes to roll down their ramps—for example, table tennis, tennis, and golf balls. Ask them how far they think the ball will roll (children can make estimates and mark them with masking tape) and whether there is any relationship between the height/length/incline of the ramp, the type of ball, and the distance the ball rolls.

3. Use adding machine tape to measure the height of the ramp and the distance the ball rolls. Record this data on the adding machine tape to provide documentation of children's investigations.

Teaching Tip

Provide pictures of castles or books about castles to inspire children's work. With David Macauley's *Castle* (Houghton Mifflin, 1982), children can watch a castle being built—brick by brick.

Surveyor's Office

Make "job" cards that invite children to measure how many blocks it takes to get from one place in the classroom to another or across an object.

1. On sentence strips, write the following sentence frame:

How many _____ to cross from
the _____ to the _____ ?

Fill in the blanks with pictures to create a task for your young surveyors—for example:

How many ⬡ to cross from the 🪑 to the 🚪 ?

2. Children select a card, complete the task, and report their findings (by counting the blocks).

3. As a variation, make several cards that vary the size of the block used to measure, while keeping what is measured the same (so children will measure the same distance with blocks of different sizes). Have "surveyor teams" order the cards from the most to the least number of blocks used. Guide children to notice that the smaller the block, the greater the number of blocks needed.

Five-Block Buildings

Constructing a building using only five blocks gives children an opportunity to construct and deconstruct the number five!

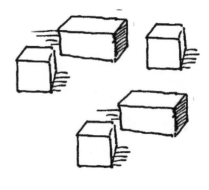

1. Have children choose two different shapes to make their buildings. (They will determine how many of each shape they need, for a total of five, as they work.) Provide paper so children can keep track of the shapes they choose and how many blocks of each shape they use.

2. When children complete their two-shape/five-block structures, guide them in describing their buildings with words and numerals—for example:

Two triangles plus three rectangles make a five-block building.
or 2 + 3 = 5

3. Display the combination sentence next to each building or next to a photograph of the building. Repeat with 10 blocks. Then try 20 (see page 63).

Twenty-Block Buildings

Each day, invite two children to become the "Twenty Block" building crew. They plan, build, and finally report on a building they construct with 20 blocks.

1. Share a rhyme to get students thinking about their block designs (see right).

2. Stock a crate with 20 blocks and a couple of hard hats. Provide materials (large-square graph paper, pencils, and so on) for documenting the building process—from planning to completion.

3. Let building crews explore the blocks in the crate, then discuss and plan their designs. Encourage creative thinking: *To make the tallest building possible, how should the blocks be arranged? How can the blocks be used to construct a building around a garden?* Graph paper can be an interesting way for children to investigate design ideas. Model how to use different combinations of graph squares to represent blocks.

4. As children build, encourage them to document the process—for example, in the form of drawings that show different stages of construction.

5. Once a team has completed a building project, it's time for a tour. Ask the members of the team what they can tell classmates about the building. *Does it have an especially sturdy base? How many blocks around is the base? How many blocks wide is the building? High? Have blocks been used in an out-of-the-ordinary way? Are there unique features?* Photograph children with their buildings, if possible, and display at the block center. Invite continued observations and discoveries about the different shapes 20 blocks can take!

Twenty Blocks

20 blocks inside this crate,
20 blocks to build something great.
20 blocks for friends to try
To make a building by and by.
When you're done we'll gather 'round
To see how you've put your blocks down.
Then a story you can tell
Of how you've built your structure well.

Measure Me

Children's masking-tape outlines are fun to explore. How many inch cubes will it take to fill in the shape? How many Unifix blocks?

1. Have children take turns lying on the floor as you outline their bodies with masking tape (or electrical tape in different colors).

2. Have children work with a partner to fill in the area of their outline. Smaller inch cubes or Unifix blocks create more precise measurements.

3. When the area is completely covered, children can count how many of each type of block they used. This is an opportunity to count by fives and tens.

Who's in the Cave?

Time to get out the jungle animals (rubber or plastic) for some exploration of size order. This activity invites children to explore size and use information they gather to match animals to homes.

1. With children, sort the animals by size (seriation). Invite related observations and comparisons—for example: *Which animal is the biggest? Which is the longest? Which one has the longest legs? Which one has the shortest ears?*

2. Let children continue with their own explorations. They can make link chains to represent the length or height of various animals. Another possibility is grouping the animals by a size attribute—for example, a group of animals less than four links long, a group of animals more than six links long.

3. After spending some time with these comparisons, let children work with a buddy to build "caves" for the animals out of blocks. Before children get started, review what they know about caves, so all children have similar knowledge to bring to their structures. Remind children to leave an opening for their animal to get in, and to make the cave wide and tall enough for their animal to fit inside. They need to make the cave not too big and not too small, but just right.

4. After placing the animals "at home" in their caves, children can let classmates guess which animal is in their cave. Guide children to notice differences in size among the caves. *How many blocks did it take to make each cave? Can you make any connections between the size of the caves and the size of the animals?*

5. To encourage ongoing learning based on these experiences, display photographs of each toy animal next to its cave. As children revisit the photographs, they will make new connections and deepen their understandings. The photographs also serve to document learning for visitors, who will enjoy hearing from children about the caves they built.

Measuring Kit: Adding Machine Tape and Other Measuring Miracles

Often children who have spent extensive time problem solving and creating in the block area have nothing tangible to show for it at the end of the day. A measuring kit provides children with the tools they need to document and share those accomplishments. To make the kit, stock a lunch box or other container with scissors, string, yarn, spools of adding machine tape, blank labels, links, cubes, paper, index cards, and writing tools. Here are some options for using the kit:

- Children can use adding machine tape as a regular method for recording nonstandard measurements of their buildings. Children can work with partners to take measurements—with one holding the adding machine tape in position while the other marks the end point (to record height, width, perimeter, and so on). Make a note about children's structures directly on the adding machine tape—for example "Kim's building was this long" or "Austin's building was this wide." Add the date, then roll up and use a paper clip to secure for easy transport home.

- Children can also take nonstandard measurements with string or yarn, cutting it to show height, length, width, perimeter, and so on. Children might like to display these measurements along with a caption that tells more about the structure.

Teaching Tip

These measurement records affirm the importance of the "work" the children are doing as they build, and will spark math-rich conversations at home.

Cleanup Graphs

Data is engaging to young children, especially when they are allowed to lead the way. The use of concrete objects, such as blocks, makes graphing rich with opportunities to observe their mathematical thinking. With graphing as a regular part of the block area cleanup procedure, children make discoveries about shapes, strengthen their sense of number, and build a foundation for data analysis.

1. To create a baseline for a graph, place one of each type of block below a strip of masking (or electrical) tape.

2. As children take apart their structures and get ready to put the blocks away, have them line up matching blocks above the tape.

3. Count and compare the blocks in each column: *How many more square blocks were used than rectangular blocks? Which block was used the least? Were any blocks used in equal amounts?*

4. As an extension, children can use the cleanup graph template (page 68) to show how many blocks they used in a structure, coloring in one square for each matching block.

65

Name _____ Date _____

 # Block Report

Builders: _____

_____

How many blocks? _____

How high? _____

How wide? _____

Special features: _____

Name _____ Date _____

Block Report

Here is a picture of my block building.

Integrating Math Into the Early Childhood Classroom   Scholastic Teaching Resources

Name _____ Date _____

Equal-Share Builders

Our blocks looked like this:

I built this:

My block buddy built this:

Integrating Math Into the Early Childhood Classroom   Scholastic Teaching Resources

Cleanup Graph

Integrating Math Into the Early Childhood Classroom   Scholastic Teaching Resources

Dramatic Play

Standards Connections

Activity	Number and Operations	Algebra	Geometry	Measurement	Data Analysis
Telephone!	•	•			
Guest Book	•	•			
Problem Solved	•	•			
Making Menus	•	•			•
Pizza, Please	•	•	•		•
It's a Buffet	•	•	•		
The Doctor Is In	•	•		•	•
Doctor's Orders	•	•		•	
Baby Measure	•	•		•	•
Measure You, Measure Me	•	•		•	•
Office Business	•	•			
Off to the Grocery Store	•	•			•
Flyer Fun	•				•
Shoe Shop	•	•		•	•
Measuring Mat		•		•	
Daily Sales	•	•			•
Taking Inventory	•	•			•
Car Care Center	•	•			
Castle Activities	•	•	•	•	•
Garden Activities	•	•	•	•	•

Dramatic play is rich in possibilities for learning math, as long as activities are planned effectively. Common office and shopping scenarios call upon children to use numbers in such diverse forms as money, telephone numbers, and hours of business. Organizing materials—from dishes to grocery items—requires classification and seriation. Matching numbers of plates to numbers of cups encourages one-to-one correspondence and counting skills.

Restaurants are natural settings for math skill development. There are parties to seat (how many in a group?) and time to keep an eye on. There are menus with prices and orders to take. Cooking in the restaurant means preparing orders in turn, following directions in recipes, setting oven temperatures, keeping track of cooking times, and counting customers and servings of different menu items. Sometimes a busy bakery or delicatessen requires that customers take a number so they can be served in an orderly manner. Pizza makers need to choose sizes and count out toppings as they fill orders.

Doctors' and veterinary offices require measuring and weighing. Even a car-care set-up requires organizing the garage and matching vehicles to keys and keys to owners. And, of course, there are always bills to pay and receipts to make! All of these are incidental to the tasks of role-playing and social interaction that are the overarching goals of the dramatic play area.

Math-Rich Materials for the Dramatic Play Area

For a home, restaurant, or grocery store:

- Baby bottles
- Bakery boxes
- Cash register
- Class phone book (see page 71)
- Crib
- Cups and saucers, or mugs (plastic)
- Dolls and doll clothes
- Foods (plastic or rubber)
- Grocery containers (empty and clean; macaroni and cheese, pasta, butter, rice, yogurt, crackers, milk and juice, dish soap, etc.)
- High chair

- Hours-of-Business sign
- Menus
- Muffin tins
- Napkins
- Order pads (pages 84, 87, 89, 108, 109)
- Pizza boxes
- Place mats (cut to appropriate size)
- Plates
- Pots and pans
- Table numbers
- Telephone
- Utensils

For a doctor's/veterinarian's office:

- Appointment book
- Bandages
- Blood pressure cuff
- Calendar
- Cash receipts
- Cash register
- Clock with office hours
- Examining room/table numbers
- "How many patients seen today?" chart

- Links
- Multilink cubes
- Otoscope (for ears)
- Pads for bills/receipts
- Pads for the doctor's orders
- Pan balance scale
- Small handheld mirror
- Stethoscope
- Teddy bear counters

Telephone!

Whether children are "calling" home or a favorite restaurant to place a takeout order, a telephone in the dramatic play area is an important tool that children never tire of using.

1. To make a class phone book, have children draw their faces on a sheet of paper, and stamp, trace, copy, or independently write their phone number at the bottom (this is a good way to find out who knows their home phone number; check with parents/guardians first before publishing any child's phone number).

2. Create a "business directory" (or add "business pages" to the class phone book) and list phone numbers for favorite places (such as restaurants and toy stores; these might be real or pretend places).

3. Encourage children to use the phone book to look up important numbers, then dial them. This gives them an opportunity to notice, match, and say numerals while at play.

4. Notice opportunities in children's phone play to make additional math connections—for example, children calling for dinner reservations can tell the maitre d' how many people are in their party and what time they would like to eat. Posting phone numbers for "takeout orders only," taxis, and other services gives children more options.

5. Store directories by the phone in the dramatic play area. Place memo paper near the phone book in case anyone wants to write down a friend's number or "take a message."

Teaching Tip

Check with parents/guardians before including children's phone numbers in the class phone book. Include a page for each child, but leave out phone numbers for children whose families prefer not to have their phone numbers published in this way.

71

Guest Book

Use a large whiteboard or a sheet of posterboard for keeping track of visitors to the class restaurant, bakery, or pizza parlor each day. Children can sign themselves in on the board (or be signed in by the establishment's "host"), and wait to be called for their table. In the meantime, this is a good opportunity to see the ways in which children use numbers to tell how long the wait might be. You can give out numbers to the people waiting as well, so they can match the number that is called with the numeral on their slip. (See Math Talk, below, for more ideas.)

Problem Solved

Restaurants have more than one table, so each table should have a numeral prominently displayed. Provide manipulatives for some restaurant-related problem solving and pose questions such as the following:

- *How many seats are there at that table? If we add a seat, will it fit a party of five?*

- *How many tables for two are there? How many can these tables seat altogether?* (Count by twos.)

- *What tables could be put together to seat a party of seven?*

- *If there are four seats at the counter and two are filled, how many are left?*

- *If all the tables are filled and one party leaves, how many tables will be available?*

Math Talk

The dramatic play restaurant area invites math-rich conversations:

- How long will I have to wait for a table?

- How many parties are ahead of us?

- How many people are in your party?

- What size pizza would you like?

- Would you like a thin or thick crust?

- How much is an extra topping?

- How many cupcakes would you like altogether?

Making Menus

When children make menus for the dramatic play area, they organize, categorize, work with numbers and money, and more.

1. To make menus, children can cut out pictures from magazines or draw foods they want to include, then arrange them on paper by categories and glue them in place. For example, one menu might be organized by Breakfast and Lunch, another by Fish, Pasta, Soup, Beverages, and Desserts.

2. Have children decide on prices for their menu items and list them accordingly. This is a good opportunity to discuss how dollar signs and decimal points are used in menus (and other places). Guide children to notice that dollars are on one side and cents on the other.

3. Before the restaurant opens, make copies of the menus, and for each set of menus make small order pads that list all the menu items, so waiters can easily tally a party's order. Or provide blank pads and let children draw pictures (or use words) to keep track of customer orders.

Pizza, Please

Have a supply of pizza-size cardboard circles on hand, along with slice-size cardboard triangles and clean pizza boxes (large and small). Children can create their dream pizzas with reusable art supplies that represent different toppings. Rather than have children glue down the toppings, just have them arrange the toppings on the pizza circles or slices to fill an order (see order form, page 84), then remove and replace them as new pizza orders arrive. (Use sticky tack to keep toppings in place.) Here are some suggestions for toppings:

- White or cream-colored yarn cut into short uneven pieces (shredded cheese)
- Red tissue paper (sauce)
- Short strips of red and green felt (peppers)
- Brown felt circles (pepperoni or sausage)
- Foam "peanuts" (onions)

Teaching Tip

In addition to or instead of the art-supply pizza toppings, make multiple copies of the Pizza Toppings reproducible on page 85 and have children help color the items and cut them out. Glue Velcro dots to the back of each topping and on the pizza circles or slices. (Laminate toppings if desired for durability.)

73

Teaching Tip

Children can work together to make an Office Hours sign to display, with the days and times that the doctor is available to see patients. They might also post a payment schedule, informing patients of office-visit costs.

It's a Buffet

Sometimes a restaurant will have a special buffet that customers can walk around, choosing what they want from the offerings. For a variation on the dramatic play restaurant theme, try a buffet setup. If each item costs one dollar and each child has five one-dollar bills, the buffet will move along smoothly and the children will have playful practice with one-to-one correspondence. To set up a buffet, simply arrange various play foods in containers or foil pans. Stack plates and utensils at one end. Place "beverages" at the other end. (Plastic or paper cups or clean, empty milk cartons work well.) Children can take turns being the cashier.

The Doctor Is In

The doctor's office is a common theme for dramatic play. There are a number of authentic math-based understandings that can develop here.

1. Spend some time during a group meeting to develop a list of "things we need for the doctor's office." Some of those items will lend themselves to further discussion involving math concepts, such as temperature, weight, and measurement. For example:

   Child: You need a thermometer.
   Teacher: How will that help?
   Child: It tells the doctor if you have a fever.
   Teacher: And what is a fever?
   Child: It's when you are hot.
   Teacher: So we can have a thermometer to tell us how hot we are.

   It will be important to then show children on a digital thermometer what the number would be if you were "hot" with a fever.

2. Discuss "office hours" (the time and days that the office is open and closed), as well as cost per visit for more math-based experiences.

Doctor's Orders

A good doctor always gives patients plenty of advice about getting better! Provide copies of the Doctor's Orders form (page 86). Encourage children to give specific instructions to their "patients" for getting better, including, for example, how many days of bed rest, how many glasses of water to drink, how many days until the patient can go back to school, work, or outside, and how many days until a follow-up visit.

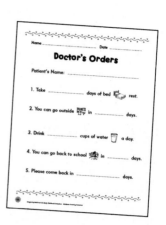

Baby Measure

Babies (dolls) being brought to the doctor's office need to be weighed and measured.

1. Stock the dramatic play center with copies of an individual height and weight chart (page 87).

2. Provide a pan balance (use cubes, counters, or other manipulatives for weight matching). For measuring length, provide yarn or string and links.

3. Demonstrate for children how to measure with both the balance and the height chart. Then when the pretend moms, dads, and other caretakers bring their babies to the doctor's, children can do the same thing, and record measurements on their baby's chart.

Measure You, Measure Me

Measure you,

Measure me,

Measuring is fun, you see.

Pick a leg, or choose a head,

Measure the part that I have said.

In addition to measuring the babies, children can pair up and take turns measuring each other.

1. Fill a basket with picture cards of body parts children can measure: leg, arm, head, finger, and so on. Children will also need string (or yarn), scissors, links, cubes, and blocks for measuring.

2. At group meeting, recite the rhyme above. Invite a volunteer to choose a card from the basket and name the part.

3. Invite a volunteer to measure with string (or yarn) the length (width, circumference) of the body part named. Children can then trade places.

4. Later, children can decide how to measure their string lengths (using cubes, links, or blocks), then display the results. Add a sign to tell what children learned about their measurements—for example, "My arm was this long, and that is the same as twenty-eight links!"

Office Business

How many patients did the doctor see today? Use a set of flip cards with numerals on them or have children make tally marks on a whiteboard to show how many patients visited the doctor's office in a day. If the visits cost $5 or $10 each, children may begin to see how that adds up as they point to each tally mark (or flip the numeral cards) and count by fives or tens.

Teaching Tip

Children can report on their measurement news at group time later in the day or the following day. (This can also be a job for the day's Count or Countess; see page 28.) This is an excellent opportunity to use math language—for example, to describe and compare the length of the two pieces of string or to discuss which measurement in links was longer or shorter.

75

Teaching Tip

Stocking the dramatic play center with small note pads invites children to give receipts when they make a sale. This provides good practice with writing money signs.

Off to the Grocery Store

Numbers abound in a grocery store, with item numbers, categories, and sales making for number-rich fun.

- Save store coupons and flyers in preparation for opening the grocery store. These are good for grocery games and displays that support a math-rich environment.

- On long tables or bookcases, sort groceries by category and use a visual cue for organizing each area: breads, canned goods, paper goods, fruits, vegetables (produce), dairy, meat, and fish.

- Collect grocery bags (big and small; paper, plastic, and cloth). Write a numeral on each bag to indicate the number of things that can go in it. Children can bag groceries accordingly (good for counting and one-to-one correspondence).

- Provide small pads of paper for making grocery lists and baskets for shopping. Add play money and a cash register and children are ready to go grocery shopping!

Flyer Fun

A stack of grocery store flyers (families can help save them) becomes a set of board games when combined with numeral cards.

1. Each child takes a flyer (his or her "game board"), one sheet only, and sits at a table. Provide a set of numeral cards 1–10 (see page 37), with duplicates of each numeral.

2. Children take turns turning over a numeral card, and putting an X on that numeral wherever it appears on the game board. For example, a child who takes the 3 card can cross out the 3 in 39 cents or the 3 in "3 for a dollar!" This creates opportunities for discussion of place value in the context of the game. If you prefer, you can cut, paste, and copy your own flyers with fewer choices on them.

Shoe Shop

Save all shoes, large, small, fancy, plain, and shoe boxes. (Families might be willing to donate both old shoes and shoe boxes.) When you open a shoe store you will need plenty of choices!

1. Gather many shoe boxes and place a pair of shoes in each.

2. Mark shoes with numbered "size" stickers and boxes with the same number to support "sales clerks" in getting the right match. These numbers don't need to correspond to actual sizes. Give each pair of shoes a different size.

3. In every shoe store there are shoes for dressing up, shoes for play, and shoes for other purposes. How many categories do children wish to have in their shoe store? Make a list and then place signs on the shelves for the types of shoes that belong there.

4. Naturally, shoes will have to be priced so that the owners can see how much money they made that day. Price shoes to support the numbers children are learning (for example, $1 to $5 or $10).

Measuring Mat

Much measuring goes on at the shoe store. Make a measuring mat for children to match up their foot size. Draw foot shapes in increasing sizes on a large sheet of posterboard. (You can write sizes on them to match the numbers on the shoe boxes.) Laminate the mat for durability. Children can match up their feet to find the size that is the best fit.

" Math Talk "

Use the shoe store to encourage children's use of language related to measurement and comparisons:

- Oh, is that one too small for your foot? Which one is bigger? Is that the biggest shoe there is?

- I wonder: Is this the right size for me or is my foot too long?

- This foot shape is big! Which one is smaller? Which is the smallest?

- Is my foot bigger or smaller than yours? How can you tell?

Daily Sales

Each morning, put up a chart to keep track of the day's sales. Children can use a bingo marker to make a stamp on the chart for each pair of shoes they sell. Set up the chart by categories (sneakers, party shoes, sandals, boots, and so on) so children can practice sorting skills as they keep track of sales. To go further, use the chart to compare the number of pairs of shoes with the number of shoes: The number of pairs will always be half the number of shoes and the number of shoes will always be twice the number of pairs. Use links to give children a concrete model for building understanding of this concept. Incorporate a daily report on shoe sales if children show an interest.

Teaching Tip

For more fun with feet, have children follow the directions on Foot Measure (page 88). They can use tracings of their shoe as a nonstandard measuring tool.

77

Collecting and
organizing data
gives children
opportunities to
develop a range
of skills—from
classifying and
categorizing to
counting and
comparing. Children
develop thinking
skills as they propose
questions for research
and analyze results.
They develop
strategies and apply
those strategies to
new problems as
they grow in their
understanding.

Taking Inventory

For more shoe store activity,
children can take inventory.
(For a reproducible inventory
form, see page 24; use as a
model to create one for shoes.)

- Line up the shoes to practice
  skip-counting by twos.
  *How many shoes are there
  altogether?* To break this
  task down into smaller pieces, inventory shoes in each category first.

- Try using a roll-out graph (see page 19) to display inventory data. Roll out as
  many graph strips as there are categories of shoes. Label each graph strip with
  a category (for example, sneakers, boots, dress-up shoes). Have children place
  a marker on the appropriate graph strip to represent each pair of shoes they
  inventory. They can count the graph squares to calculate and compare category
  totals. Ask: *Do you have a bigger inventory of sneakers or boots? Are you
  running low on shoes in any categories? How can you tell?*

Car Care Center

The care and maintenance of vehicles is both interesting to and engaging for
young children, and creating and running a shop involves a number of math
investigations.

- Set up a car care center with numbered bays for workspaces. Stock the center
  with rags and spray bottles filled with water (label them). Number the rags
  and spray bottles to match the work bays (one set for each bay).

- Make numbered name tags for car care experts to write their names on and wear.
  (Have tag numbers match the bay numbers where children will do their work.)

- Number vehicles (toy cars and other toy vehicles) scheduled for servicing (with
  numbers matching the bays in which they will be serviced). Create a schedule
  to build in opportunities to learn about time (measurement) and order (first,
  second, third).

- The cleanup crew can wash each vehicle after service, using, of course, the
  numbered cloth and spray bottle that matches the designated bay and car!

- Invoices let children record such information on cars as the owner's name and
  phone number. When servicing is complete, they can itemize repairs and list
  fees for their services.

Life in a Castle

Castles engage children in a life of long ago, and invite math connections in a cross-curricular approach to learning. Here are some ideas to set the stage.

- Children can create castle walls by forming patterns with rectangle construction-paper "stones" on large sheets of posterboard (or an appliance box, opened like a "room divider"). How many stones does a child need to cover one area of a wall (or board)?

- For future architects in your class, provide many, many shapes of paper in varying sizes and colors. Children can arrange them on a large sheet of construction paper and glue them in place to create their own castle designs.

- The cook works inside the castle walls to provide meals for the castle community living there, creating opportunities for following directions. *How much bread does the castle cook need to feed everyone? How about berries, nuts, and cheese?*

Counting With the King and Queen

A castle is a good place for a king and queen to live, and counting is something they can do a lot of. There are jewels to count, also coins and other treasures.

1. Let children help fill "treasure chest" posterboards with jewels, coins, and other treasures. Label posters by categories and let children decorate them accordingly. For example, the "Queen's Jewels" poster will need sequins and craft-store jewels of all shapes, sizes, and colors, as well as necklaces, rings (pictures are fine), and a cardboard crown or two. The "King's Coins" poster can be filled with stamped coins, foil gold coins, paper circles painted silver and gold, and photos of coins from magazines.

2. Make a copy of the Counting With the King and Queen record sheet (page 89). Children can represent their counting in a treasure chest on this record sheet in a way that is appropriate to their abilities, by using tallies, marks, representations, or numerals. For example, students might tally the queen's jewels by color, or the king's coins by type.

Create a Crown

The king and queen need crowns for every occasion. Royalty can order crowns daily by filling out the Crown Order Form (page 89), stating how many of each crown decoration they would like (sequins, ribbons, glitter, stickers, and so on). This will tell the royal subjects how many of each to count out and use when they fill an order. Children can take turns being royalty and royal subjects so everyone can order and create a crown at some point.

Castle Time: Week of Rhyme

To go with a castle theme at the dramatic play area, "Sing a Song of Sixpence" is a just-right rhyme to share. Here, with each day of the week comes a different part of the rhyme, along with a corresponding hands-on activity. Copy the entire rhyme on sentence strips to use with a pocket chart, or write the rhyme on a flip chart and display at an easel. As you recite the rhyme with children each day, take opportunities to play with language (including rhyming words) and make natural math connections as they arise.

Day 1

Sing a song of sixpence

A pocket full of rye;

Four and twenty blackbirds

Baked in a pie.

Recite these first four lines of the rhyme with children. Using sturdy paper (laminate if desired), cut out "pockets" of various sizes and shapes and punch holes for lacing along the edges. Provide children with pockets and yarn and let them stitch up "a pocket full of rye." Ask: *How many sides are on a pocket? How many pockets are on your own clothing?*

Day 2

When the pie was opened

The birds began to sing.

Now, wasn't that a dainty dish to

Set before the king?

Revisit and recite the first four lines of the rhyme (day 1), then add four new lines. Play with new rhyming words for *sing* and *king.* Then let each child bake four and twenty blackbirds (raisins) in a pie made with crescent roll or biscuit dough. (Check for food allergies first.) Use counters to model counting on from 20 to add 4 more. Ask: *How many blackbirds were singing?*

Day 3

The king was in his counting house
Counting out his money;

Recite the first two portions of the rhyme (days 1 and 2), then add on the next two lines. Next, visit the castle's "counting house" to sort and count jewels and coins. Or give children small cups filled with assorted coins to sort and count.

Day 4

The queen was in the parlor
Eating bread and honey

Recite the rhyme for days 1–4 with children. Can children find two new rhyming words? (*money* and *honey*) What other words rhyme with these? (Don't worry about spelling patterns here; just focus on rhymes. So children might rhyme *bunny, funny,* and *sunny.*) Use cookie cutters to make shapes of bread to toast and top with jelly, cream cheese, or other spreads. (Check for food allergies first.)

Day 5

The maid was in the garden,
Hanging out the clothes
Along came a blackbird and
Snipped off her nose!

Make this a wash day for the doll clothes. After children wash the clothes (in wash basins), string up a clothesline and let children use clothespins (good for fine motor development) to hang up the clothes to dry, organizing them by any attribute they choose (for example, type, size, or color).

Garden Center

A garden center perks up a room as spring arrives and provides many opportunities for counting, classifying, comparing, measuring, and more.

- Flowers (plastic) invite sorting by color, size, and variety. Children can determine prices and fill orders. Naturally there will be an exchange of money and perhaps a tally of flowers sales each day. New flowers may arrive from the flower market; children can check them in, counting and recording how many of each type arrived.

- Every garden center should have a seed planting area where, for a small "fee," children can purchase a cup, several scoops of potting soil, and seeds of their choice. Prepare an illustrated sign with a sequence of steps for children to follow. (See sample, above.) Following steps in order helps children develop organizational skills while utilizing math.

Class Flower Catalog

Every good garden shop has a catalog to show its beautiful blossoms. Children can create a classroom catalog organized by color.

1. Invite children to choose a color, then cut out flowers of that color from magazines or flower catalogs.

2. Have children glue their flowers to a sheet of construction paper, then count the flowers and write or stamp the numeral on the paper.

3. To make a class flower catalog, put children's pages together. (Bind with O-rings to make it easy to turn the pages and add new ones.) For sorting practice before you bind the pages, have children organize flower pages by color, grouping different tones of each color together. Children may even wish to assign a price to their blossoms and note that information on the page.

Ten-Petal Posies

With a ten frame and two colors of tissue paper circles, children can play a game that lets them create festive posies from petals they choose—and build number sense at the same time.

1. In preparation for this game, cut out tissue-paper circles in two colors. (Stack the paper to cut many circles at once; use a lid as a pattern.) Make a set of counting cards consisting of numerals 1, 2, and 3 (page 37) and ten frames (enlarge the template on page 40 or draw ten frames on large sheets of paper).

2. Give each child a cup, a pipe cleaner, and a ten frame. Stack the counting cards facedown.

3. Let children take turns selecting a card, then choosing that many tissue circles and placing them on the ten frame (one petal per section). Continue until children have filled all ten sections with a petal.

4. Before they put their posies together, have children color each square of their ten frame to represent their colors. This is a good way to compare two numbers: "I have more pink than purple." "I have two blue and eight yellow."

5. To put the posies together, have children stack their tissue paper circles. Use a large needle (teacher use only) to make two holes near the center of each child's stack of circles. Have children push one end of the pipe cleaner through a hole and the other end through the remaining hole, line up each half on the other side, and twist to make the stem. Then children can gently pull up on each tissue paper circle to create their posy petals.

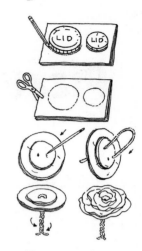

Counting on Tulips

Plant a garden of tulips with an art activity that supports counting by ones, fives, and tens.

1. Display a length of mural paper, and set out containers of paint in different colors.

2. Have children paint the palms of their hands, then stamp their hands on the paper (some distance above the base of the paper), with fingers pointing up and close together.

3. After the handprints are dry, children can paint in stems and leaves.

4. Then have some counting fun. Children can count each flower (by ones), and petals (by fives) and record all findings.

Circle Flowers

Circles can inspire children to create colorful fields of flowers that promote problem solving.

1. Cut out many circles of paper in varying sizes and colors. Place an assortment of circles in plastic storage bags or envelopes (one for each child).

2. Give each child a bag of circles and a sheet of paper. Have children experiment with arranging the circles on the paper—for example, from biggest to smallest, or by color. When they are satisfied with their arrangements, they can glue the circles on the paper. The circles become the centers of flowers, to which children can add petals, leaves, stems, and other details.

Name _____ Date _____

Pizza Parlor Order Form

_____  Cheese

_____ Mushrooms

_____ Peppers

_____ Onions

_____ Pepperoni

_____ Sausage

Integrating Math Into the Early Childhood Classroom   Scholastic Teaching Resources

Pizza Toppings

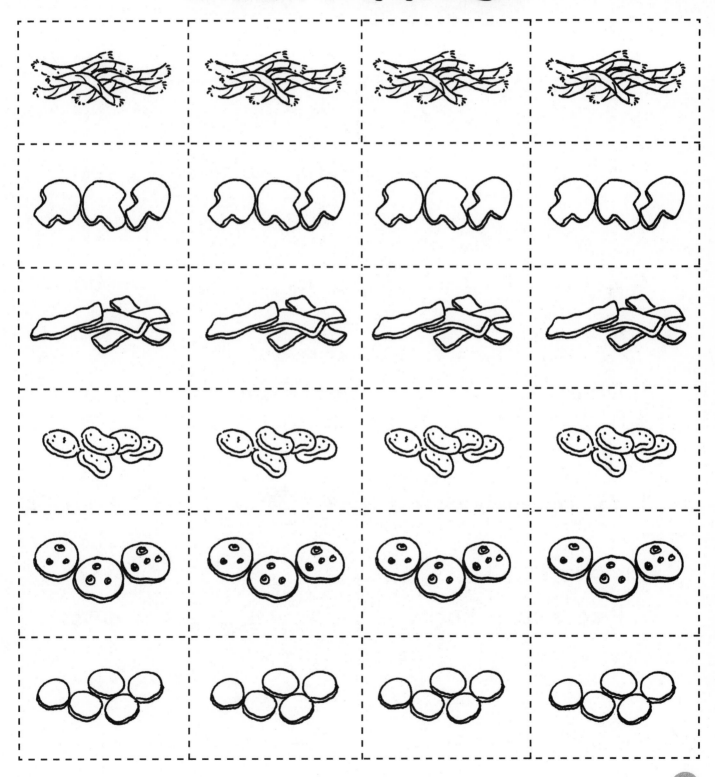

Integrating Math Into the Early Childhood Classroom Scholastic Teaching Resources

Name _____   Date _____

Doctor's Orders

Patient's Name: _____

1. Take _____ days of bed 🛏 rest.

2. You can go outside 🛝 in _____ days.

3. Drink _____ cups of water 🥛 a day.

4. You can go back to school 🏫 in _____ days.

5. Please come back in _____ days.

Integrating Math Into the Early Childhood Classroom   Scholastic Teaching Resources

Name _____ Date _____

Baby Measure

Baby, baby very small,

Baby, baby very tall,

Baby heavy or baby light

All the babies feel just right!

Baby's Name: _____

Length: _____

Weight: _____

Other Comments: _____

_____

Next Appointment: _____

Integrating Math Into the Early Childhood Classroom   Scholastic Teaching Resources

Name _____ Date _____

Foot Measure

Get some paper. Get a pen.

Trace your shoe from end to end.

Cut it out and write your name,

In case a friend's is just the same.

Then you're set to start the fun—

Measure by feet, one by one.

What I Measured	How Many Feet
1.	
2.	
3.	
4.	
5.	

Integrating Math Into the Early Childhood Classroom   Scholastic Teaching Resources

Name _____ Date _____

Counting With the King and Queen

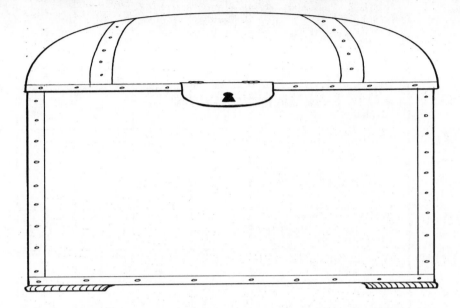

Name _____ Date _____

Crown Order Form

_____ sequins and jewels

_____ glitter glue dabs

_____ ribbons

_____ stickers

Integrating Math Into the Early Childhood Classroom Scholastic Teaching Resources

Art Activities

Standards Connections

Activity	Number and Operations	Algebra	Geometry	Measurement	Data Analysis
Shapes, Shapes, and More Shapes			•		
Ticket to Art	•	•	•		
Paper-Chain Math Explorations	•	•	•	•	•
Binocular Observations			•		•
Necklace Math	•	•	•	•	
Snow Children	•	•	•	•	•
Gingerbread Boys and Girls	•	•	•		•
A Pair Is Two . . . Two to a Pair	•	•	•		•
Baa, Baa, Black Sheep	•	•	•		
Symmetry Paper-Folding Art			•		
Clickety Clack Down the Track	•	•	•		
Twinkle, Twinkle, Little Star	•		•		
Going on Vacation	•	•	•		•
Construction Area: Hard Hats Allowed	•		•	•	•
Art Shopping	•	•	•		•
Shape Vehicles	•	•	•	•	
What Can You Make of It?			•		

Art is an area rarely connected to math yet it connects in so many ways. Size, shape, orientation, and balance are all a part of artistic exploration and discovery. Allowing children an opportunity to experiment is essential; infusing art with math is both natural and enriching.

The art area should always offer children some "free art" materials to take and create with as they wish. These materials can and should be changed regularly with some specific theme in mind. That theme could be shape, size, texture, or even structure. Children learn about geometry as they place two right triangles together to make a square or two squares together to make a rectangle. They learn about number when they create a pattern across a paper and run out of space to complete it at the end. They learn about dimension when they try to find just the right piece of paper to place on the top of a collage tower.

The conversations that follow an art experience provide children with opportunities to develop mathematical language as they explain how they formed a two-colored square with two triangles or how many pieces it took to create that colorful flower. When recording children's comments and stories about their artwork, always use a separate sheet of paper. After all, nobody wrote a story on a Renoir! We want to value the art for its own sake.

Shapes, Shapes, and More Shapes

Art paper for painting, collage, and drawing doesn't always need to be in the form of the standard rectangular sheets children expect to see. For an interesting change, stock art areas with paper cut into various shapes. Try circles for the easel, triangles for a collage station, and narrower rectangular strips to go with the marker box. The shapes you choose for each art area aren't as important as the variation you provide. As your young artists reach into the shelf for paper to use with their markers, and pull out long, narrow strips rather than the standard sheets, they will approach their project with a fresh perspective, which will influence the art they create.

"Our initial evidence indicates that geometry and patterning are foundational for mathematics learning. They are important in and of themselves. They build on the interests and competencies of young children. Finally, they support the learning of other mathematical topics, such as number (from counting the sides of shapes to seeing numbers in rows and columns)."

(Sarama & Clements, 2004)

Ticket to Art

When children choose materials to create a structure or collage, they may do so randomly. Building in a set number of items to a project gives children a chance to think carefully about their choices and to count out their selections.

1. To introduce this activity to children, begin with a ten-piece project. Write the numeral 10 on a set of "tickets." Let children take a ticket as they prepare to begin an art project.

2. Have children choose materials to match the quantity shown on the ticket. This gives them both opportunities to count ten items in a set and to think critically about how they want to combine art materials.

3. After children complete their projects, allow time for sharing. Comparing the items they chose and the different ways they used them provides children with rich language experiences, and lets them discover that the quantity 10 can take all sorts of shapes and sizes.

4. Once children understand the process for this activity, build in increasingly complex choices. Continue to make comparisons to encourage connections—for example, compare the results of a 10-piece project with a 20-piece project!

Paper-Chain Math Explorations

Paper chains are engaging because they are three-dimensional and grow so very long. Following are some fun suggestions for using paper chains for math explorations:

- Invite children to use two colors and notice the patterns that emerge.

- Challenge children to find something in the room exactly the same length as a chain they create.

- Try having everyone make a ten-link chain. Invite children to imagine how long the chain would be if they connected all of their chains. Discuss objects that might be as long as (or shorter than) the class chain: *Would one side of the classroom be longer or shorter than the chain? Would the chain be shorter than or longer than the slide?* Try it out! Making predictions such as these allows children to think about problem solving rather than focus only on the physical action of linking the chain to another object.

Binocular Observations

Young children can transform masking tape and cardboard tubes into almost anything. With this art project, tubes become binoculars for a number hunt.

1. Help children tape two bathroom-tissue tubes together in binocular fashion. Punch a hole in each tube (at one end of the binoculars). Attach a length of yarn to make a strap. Then let children decorate their binoculars as they wish.

2. Take a shape-exploration walk and see what shapes children can spot. Or look for numbers. Record children's observations and revisit them after the walk. Were there more rectangles or circles? Which shape did they see more of? Fewer of? Did they find an equal number of anything? *More, less,* and *equal* are critical vocabulary for math conversations and explanations. This activity will give children plenty of opportunities to use these descriptive words.

Necklace Math

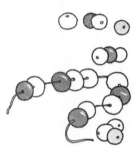

Necklaces made up of beads in different shapes and sizes give children a lot to talk about as they string.

1. Stock a center with necklace-making materials, including yarn for stringing and beads in many shapes, sizes, and colors. Don't forget to include those elliptical shapes (also known as ovals) in necklace-making materials.

2. Encourage mathematical connections as children string beads. When children ask for the "red triangle" or the "blue seven," for example, they're practicing mathematical language. When they string alternating short and long beads, they're exploring patterns. When they notice they need just a few more to make the necklace fit, they're investigating measurement. They might also count beads in necklaces by attributes: *How many red? How many round? How many big beads? Little beads?* On another day, children might enjoy stringing patterns and comparing one with another. *Which pattern uses the fewest color choices? Which uses the most? How many yellow beads are used on a string with a yellow, blue, red pattern compared with a yellow, yellow, blue pattern?*

"Math Talk"

As children string beads, notice the shapes they're using. Ask, for example, *Do you have a square? What can you tell me about your shape?* When working with shapes, use the actual geometric terminology as much as possible so that children feel comfortable with that mathematical language. For sample conversation starters related to shape explorations, see the reproducible Math Talk question card on page 22.

Snow Children

Winter is a perfect time to create
a class of snow children, good for
exploring shapes, practicing counting,
and sorting by categories.

1. Everyone needs a small, medium,
   and large circle of white paper
   for the body. Children can glue
   their circles in order on a sheet of
   paper, then glue on features, such
   as eyes, nose, ears, buttons, hat,
   and scarf. (Provide construction
   paper, ribbon, and other collage
   materials.)

2. When the glue is dry, let children sort and re-sort their snow children by
   different categories. *Are there more snow children with hats or scarves? How
   many buttons do the snow children have altogether?* Perhaps children will
   have their own investigative questions as well.

Gingerbread Boys and Girls

After reading a story about the gingerbread boy, such as Jan Brett's *Gingerbread
Baby* (Putnam, 1999) try making some gingerbread children. This creates a
delicious springboard for exploring arrays (how many rows, how many in each
row), counting, skip-counting (how many eyes, ears, arms, buttons, and so
on), sorting (buttons, no buttons), and more. (Check for food allergies before
proceeding.)

1. Mix up gingerbread dough, and give each child a piece to roll out and cut with
   a cookie cutter. Provide raisins for eyes, nose, mouth, buttons, and so on. (For
   more information about mathematical connections with cooking, see Cooking
   Activities, pages 99–109.)

2. Arrange cookies on a baking sheet in an array (such as two by four). Before
   baking, invite children to describe what they notice about the rows (each row
   has the same number of cookies in it). Count the cookies, first by ones and
   then by another number (such as twos). Compare the total number of cookies
   with the number of students. *Is it the same? More? Less?*

3. Bake as directed. When the cookies are cool, children can sort by attributes,
   order by size (if they used different-size cookie cutters), count in turn to find
   out how many gingerbread eyes (ears, and so on) there are, and even pair up
   to share and compare cookies. Ask: *Does each cookie have two eyes? The
   same number of buttons? What's the same? What's different?*

4. Children can reproduce these gingerbread cookie arrays with sponges precut in the shape of gingerbread boys and girls. They can stamp their gingerbread children on construction-paper cookie sheets (gray or black), then decorate them just like their cookies. You might ask: *How many sponge-stamped gingerbread boys and girls are there on individual cookie sheets? How many did the whole class make altogether? How many buttons? How many eyes?*

A Pair Is Two . . . Two to a Pair

Cut out oversize mitten shapes from construction paper. Then two children at a time can create a "follow the leader" painting on the mittens.

1. One child paints a color on part of one mitten and the other child copies that on the other mitten. Then the first child paints another part with the same or another color, and the "follower" copies as before. They continue in this way until the mittens are complete.

2. When the mittens are dry, punch holes in them and string them together with a piece of crepe paper or yarn and display. This will create a pair of mittens. As the display grows, try some counting: *How many pairs? How many mittens? How many children with warm hands?*

Baa, Baa, Black Sheep

Make a bag full of soft "wool" to go with a favorite nursery rhyme.

Baa, baa, black sheep,

Have you any wool?

Yes, sir, yes, sir, three bags full.

One for my master, one for the dame,

And one for the little boy who lives down the lane.

1. Cut out small, medium, and large bag shapes (from construction paper). Fill a container with cotton balls.

2. Have each child choose a "bag," predict how many cotton balls he or she will need to fill the bag, and count out that many.

3. Children can glue the cotton balls on their bags, revising their thinking as they go. Ask: *Does it look like you will have enough? Too much?* Children can get more cotton balls as needed (or share extras with a classmate who needs more).

Teaching Tip

How many mittens for three kittens? This is a good time to share the Mother Goose rhyme "Three Little Kittens." Pair the classic version with Paul Galdone's spirited retelling, *Three Little Kittens* (Clarion, 1988), which features a cast of lively cat characters. Illustrations full of delightful details invite new discoveries with every reading.

Symmetry Paper-Folding Art

Symmetry and art are closely connected. Experimenting with symmetry in their art helps children develop concepts in geometry, including that the two halves of a symmetrical design are identical in size and shape. To create simple symmetrical designs, have children fold paper in half, then open it. Have children use eyedroppers to drop paint on one side (half) of the paper, then refold the paper, press the sides together, and rub. What do children notice when they open up their papers?

Clickety Clack Down the Track

When exploring a unit on transportation, you may want to make a sturdy wooden track for bulletin-board trains.

1. Give children craft sticks and let them play with track making for a couple of days.

2. When children have developed a plan, place roll paper on the floor or a table, and let them glue their track pieces together. It is best to do this work in a place where the track doesn't have to be moved until it is completely dry.

3. Staple the track in sections to the bulletin board. Let children count to see how much track the train crew laid altogether, then add construction-paper train cars to complete the display.

Twinkle, Twinkle, Little Star

Share a favorite rhyme, then let children count stars in their own night skies.

Twinkle, twinkle, little star,
How I wonder what you are.
Up above the world so high,
Like a diamond in the sky,
Twinkle, twinkle, little star,
How I wonder what you are.

1. Give children black paper, glue, and glitter. Model how to make dots of glue on the paper, then sprinkle the glue dots with glitter to make stars. Add other features to the starry night scene as you wish.

2. Then let children create their own starry night-sky pictures. Ask: *How many stars are there in your sky? Do you think there are more than ten? Twenty? Thirty?* In addition to counting the stars, children can count how many small, medium, and large stars they have in their skies. To keep track of their counting, children can use sticky notes. Also try sorting starry night pictures by attributes, such as least/most star coverage.

Teaching Tip

Share books about trains with children, then invite them to generate a list of types of train cars they can add to their bulletin-board train track—for example, flatcars, hopper cars, refrigerator cars, passenger cars, cargo cars, cattle cars, tank cars, and boxcars. This is a good opportunity for classification as well! When the train is complete, don't forget to count the wheels!

Going on Vacation

Is vacation approaching? Make big suitcases by cutting open brown grocery bags along the sides. Add a string or ribbon handle at the top, tie or tape on luggage tags (made from tagboard) with addresses, phone numbers, and add other details as desired. Children can "fill" their suitcases by gluing in catalog pictures or pictures from newspaper flyers. They can approach this in numerous ways—for example, by arranging pictures by category (shirts in one area, socks in another area, and so on), by color, or randomly. When children are finished, invite them to discuss what they packed (categories) and how many things they packed altogether. Then they can close up their suitcases and "go on vacation."

Construction Area: Hard Hats Allowed

Put on a hard hat for a construction project that connects counting with geometry and measurement.

1. Collect lots of paper tubes and boxes of many sizes and shapes.

2. Let children use masking tape to build with them and create structures.

3. When the structures are complete, let children measure them with links or string. They can measure one aspect of the structure with links, then the same aspect with another tool. So many sizes will emerge for the exact same length! (See Math Talk, below, for more information.)

4. This is a good opportunity to have students practice using tallies to record how many of each building material was used on their job site (for example, how many bathroom-tissue tubes, paper-towel tubes, gift-wrap tubes, jewelry boxes, cereal boxes, and shoe boxes).

 Math Talk

It is important to help children see that the size of the unit they use for measuring determines the total number of units needed to measure a given length. So if they measure a structure with links and then with a shoe, the number of links will exceed the number of shoe lengths. To help children consider this, ask:

- What was the longest (or shortest) part of the building you measured?

- How high was the section you measured? Was it the same number of cubes as links?

- Is there anything in our classroom that is as long as the longest part of the building? Take a string of links or a strip of cubes and try it out. Let me know what you find!

Art Shopping

Turn the art area into an Art Shop that reinforces counting and money skills.

1. Cut off one end section (two cups) from an egg carton to create a ten-frame egg carton. Make several of these. Gather a collection of collage materials (different papers, ribbons, foil, tissue paper, wrapping paper, packing peanuts, and so on). Place pennies in a box or other container. You might also provide shopping bags in which children can place their "purchases."

2. When children visit the Art Shop, have them place a penny in each cup of the ten-frame egg carton, and then go shopping! One penny will buy one piece of collage material. After purchasing ten items, children can go back to create a masterpiece. If the need for more materials arises, children can return to the Art Shop for more supplies (repeating the process with the pennies).

3. At the end of the day, have children help you count up those pennies to see how much the Art Shop earned.

Shape Vehicles

Simply cutting construction paper shapes in a range of sizes sets the stage for some geometric exploration. Using rectangles, squares, triangles, ellipses, and circles, children can create almost any vehicle—from a truck to a rocket.

1. Provide plenty of paper shapes in different sizes and colors.

2. As children choose and manipulate the shapes to get their vehicles just right, encourage conversations that incorporate shape names.

3. When children have completed their vehicles and glued the shapes in place, let them sort and count how many land, water, and sky vehicles they've made. They can organize the vehicles on the floor to create a graph showing how many of each type. Label the graph to make connections to the words used to describe their vehicles.

4. Children can also compare how many of each shape they used to create their vehicles. Make a record sheet by drawing the shapes on a sheet of paper. Children can use tallies to record how many of each shape they used.

What Can You Make of It?

This is a challenge activity for art. Give children an envelope with two to four shapes inside. The challenge for each child is to make a picture utilizing the shapes in the envelope. Some children will make two or more objects, while others will incorporate all of the shapes in one picture. Either approach requires some problem-solving skills. However children choose to work with the shapes, they can use markers to fill in picture details.

Teaching Tip

Introduce the Shape Vehicles activity in a group meeting to have children model their thinking as they create ideas and express them to the class.

Cooking Activities

Standards Connections					
Activity	Number and Operations	Algebra	Geometry	Measurement	Data Analysis
Build a Recipe	•	•	•	•	•
Quick-and-Easy Snacks	•	•	•	•	•
"Time" to Cook	•			•	•
How Many Cookies on a Cookie Sheet?	•	•	•	•	
Tea Party	•	•	•		
Plenty of Pancakes	•	•	•	•	•
Class Cookbook	•			•	
Count and Stir	•				
Stone Soup	•	•		•	
Vegetable and Fruit Tasting Party	•	•	•	•	•
Oceans Away	•	•			
Digging in Dirt	•	•			
Ice Cream Sundae Party	•	•	•	•	•

Teaching Tip

For all cooking activities with children, check for food allergies first. Check all ingredients as well for any that may not be suitable due to allergy restrictions.

Cooking has natural math connections. It is built on skills of measurement, quantity, capacity, and time. Children naturally develop understanding as they use measuring tools and fill cake pans, cookie sheets, and soup pots. They count ingredients, set timers, talk about oven temperature, and follow multistep directions. There are also opportunities to problem solve when things don't come out "even" or when something goes wrong. Cooking offers learning opportunities whether or not the product is a success.

Children's ability to use measuring language appropriately and their corresponding ability to understand the different terms' meanings comes in stages. Exploration and instruction in the early grades build familiarity so that later concepts can be developed on a strong foundation. To support this process, it is important to discuss key information in cooking activities before actual cooking begins. Introduce measuring tools, such as measuring cups and spoons, and allow for open exploration so children can begin to appreciate the difference in size, for example, between a ½-cup measuring cup and a 1-cup measuring cup. It's important to demonstrate, for example, that four ¼-cup measuring cups fill a 1-cup measuring cup (two ½-cup measuring cups fill it, and so on). Similarly, children should be given a chance to understand why we fill a ½-cup measuring cup all the way to the top when a recipe calls for half a cup of water.

A combination of exploration, explicit teaching, and reviewing will help teachers reach the greatest number of children in order to solidify their understanding of these key concepts.

Setting Up a Cooking Area

Set up the cooking area with a pegboard or other device on which to hang cooking tools. Label places for measuring cups with the appropriate fractions. Order whisks, spatulas, and mixing spoons by size so that children can refer to them with the appropriate attribute and so the area can be cleaned up in an organized fashion. Similarly, arrange bowls and cookie sheets by size.

Make timers and clocks available for children in the cooking area. Offer information on the length of time for the cooking and the temperature to help children develop reference points, so that the mathematical language always sounds familiar to them even if their understanding isn't fully developed. "These cupcakes will need 12 minutes at 350 degrees. That will be a very hot oven!"

Build a Recipe

Creating a recipe of their own gives children a sense of ownership about the outcome. One easy option for this kind of cooking activity wis trail mix.

1. Arrange a number of ingredients in bowls, buffet style. Suitable ingredients for trail mix include cold cereal, raisins, dried cranberries and cherries, nuts, pretzels, and sunflower seeds. (Check for allergy restrictions before choosing ingredients.)

2. Provide copies of the Build a Recipe template (page 108), modifying it as necessary to match the ingredients you choose. Also provide various measuring spoons at each ingredient station and resealable bags in which children can place their ingredients.

3. Let each child determine a recipe for trail mix and complete their Build a Recipe sheet.

4. Children can then follow their recipe to mix up a batch of trail mix to enjoy.

Quick-and-Easy Snacks

These no-cook snacks invite investigations into counting (including skip-counting), measuring, shape identification, and more.

Ants on a Log

This recipe is excellent for easy assembly at snack time.

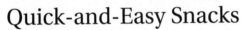

1. Cut celery into three-inch lengths (or use pretzel logs).

2. Have children spread cream cheese or peanut butter (be careful of peanut and other food allergies) on the celery or pretzels, then count out five or ten raisins (ants) and place them on the "log."

3. Together, count the raisins by fives or tens.

Shape Snacks

Cookie cutters turn bread into snacks that inspire mathematical explorations.

1. Provide children with sliced bread and various cookie cutters.

2. Let children cut out shapes and top them with peanut butter, jelly, cream cheese, or other toppings. (Watch for peanut and other food allergies.)

3. Before children enjoy their snacks, take a few minutes to identify different shapes, and count the number of peanut butter (jelly, cream cheese) shapes.

Teaching Tip

Use food coloring to turn cream cheese into a rainbow of toppings. Children can count how many shapes they have in each color.

Teaching Tip

It can be worthwhile to compare and contrast different versions of a recipe. Here are some foods that can be made in a number of ways:

- Applesauce
- Cranberry sauce
- Breads
- Chocolate chip cookies
- Macaroni and cheese

"Time" to Cook

Cooking areas offer opportunities to explicitly teach time—not to tell time, but to begin to build some understanding of time vocabulary and see ways in which time is measured. Here are ways to do this:

- Use a play clock to let children see the segments of the hour represented by lines and numbers. What part of the hour does the cooking time represent?

- Color sections of a whiteboard clock to visually represent the "block" of time needed to cook soup or bake cookies.

- Display cooking time—as a numeral and as a number word for minutes (for example, "cook for 10/ten minutes"). Set a timer so children know when that period of time as passed. (This gives children a chance to experience elapsed time.)

How Many Cookies on a Cookie Sheet?

Before making cookies, add a cookie sheet to the play-clay area so children can experiment with the number of cookies it takes to fill the cookie sheet (see Gingerbread Boys and Girls, page 94). This is helpful for developing concepts related to number, area, and estimation. Document children's understanding so you can help to refine their thinking and they can come to the cooking activity having built some understanding of these concepts.

After establishing a reliable number of cookies for one cookie sheet, use varying sizes of cookie sheets to determine if children are able to adapt their thinking. Ask children to compare the sizes of the two sheets and predict whether more or fewer cookies will fit on the new sheet. This conversation can also take place during group meeting so children can learn from the experiences of their peers.

 Math Talk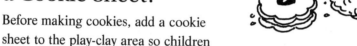

To help children use what they know to refine predictions, ask questions that focus their attention on key information:

- How many cookies do you think will fit on this cookie sheet?
- Is this new cookie sheet bigger or smaller than this one?
- Will this cookie sheet hold more or less than this cookie sheet? What do you think?

Tea Party

Making tea sandwiches is an engaging no-cook activity. These small, finger-size sandwiches offered at "tea parties" give children a chance to incorporate size, shape, and number into one activity.

1. Let children cut sliced bread into small strips or use cookie cutters to make bread shapes. Offer various types of bread—for example, white, rye, and wheat. Toast if desired.

2. Have children spread on fillings such as cream cheese, jelly, peanut butter, and sunflower butter. Other fillings can be added as desired, such as tuna fish, cucumbers, and celery. (As always, check for allergies first.)

3. Children can match tea sandwiches by types of bread, and count the number of sandwiches, different shapes, and bread types. This also works with children making their own tea sandwich recipes or taking "orders" from their friends who have filled out a Tea Party Order Form (page 108).

Plenty of Pancakes

A pancake party is always a welcome treat on a cold, dark winter's day.

1. Leading up to the party, let children experiment with paper chains to see the total number of pancakes needed for the pancake party. Allow children to offer several ideas for the number of pancakes they think they will want to eat or need to cook. (This might bring in ideas about the size of the pancakes, for example, each child would need fewer pancakes if the pancakes are larger.)

2. Have paper strips ready, and during choice time (or Morning Meeting) let children each make a paper chain to show how many pancakes they think they will eat. (Or have children add to one chain to show how many pancakes the whole class will eat.)

3. Display the lengths of children's individual paper chains (write their names on them) so they can visually observe the difference in lengths. On Pancake Party Day children can create new chains (in a different color) to show what they actually ate. Prompt children to compare: *How many in each chain? Did you think you would eat more/fewer pancakes than you did?*

4. For another comparison, put children's chains together to make two big chains (one for a total of how many they thought they would eat and one for a total of how many they did eat).

Teaching Tip

Packaged cooking products that make for good mathematical cooking include:

- Pancake mix (number, size, and problem solving)

- Gelatin or pudding (measuring and problem solving)

- Popcorn (comparing amounts—unpopped versus popped—and measuring time)

- Vegetable soups (counting and sorting)

- Trail mix (counting and sorting)

- Fruit or vegetable snacks (counting, sorting, and gathering data)

Here are two favorite versions of the "Stone Soup" story:

Stone Soup by Macia Brown (Aladdin, 1997): This Caldecott-winning retelling of the classic French tale was first published in 1947 and remains a favorite.

Stone Soup by Tony Ross (Puffin, 1992): A big, bad wolf makes an appearance in this lively version of the familiar folktale.

Class Cookbook

Throughout the year, invite family members to visit and share (or send in) favorite recipes with children. Record the recipes as they are shared, adding visuals to represent quantity, including numbers of cups and teaspoons. Organize recipes in a binder to make a "favorite recipes" book children can revisit and read again and again.

Count and Stir

When following recipes with stirring or mixing involved, assign children a number of stirs to complete before passing the bowl to the next child. This counting keeps children focused on the task of stirring and provides needed counting practice. Children count to the target number and pass the bowl until everyone has had a turn. Counting down from the target number helps develop number skills as well.

Stone Soup

Share the story "Stone Soup" (one of your favorite retellings, or try one suggested in the Teaching Tip, left). Then re-create the story with your own "stone" soup.

1. Choose a variety of vegetables, including some that children suggest and others that they may be tasting for the first time.

2. Provide safe cutting tools and surfaces, and have children cut up the ingredients, offering assistance as needed. Integrate numbers into this cooking experience—for example, having children cut sticks of celery into ten pieces per stick to provide practice in counting to ten. If you want them to practice counting backward, start children by saying ten and then cutting and counting backward until they get to one.

3. Have children place cut vegetables in small transparent containers (all the same size). Children can then observe how ten pieces of celery might take up more/less of the cup than ten pieces of zucchini. Count by tens as you add the vegetables to the soup pot and see how many pieces there are altogether.

4. When you've wrapped up the math explorations, cook the soup as directed in the recipe you are using. If you wish to do a fast soup method, start with vegetable broth instead of water as a base.

Vegetable and Fruit Tasting Party

A vegetable or fruit tasting party is a math-rich experience as long as teachers purposefully plan for opportunities to observe, compare, and count.

1. When planning the tasting party, bring in a variety of vegetables (or fruit) for children to sort. Children can use place mats for this. Allow the sorting and discussion to originate with children. If a child can articulate a reason to group vegetables together, allow that group to be formed. Children can sort all red foods, all long foods, all bumpy foods, or any other interesting group that comes to mind. Take this opportunity to count and compare groups.

2. Create measure and sort mats for prep work. To make measure mats, draw several lines of varying lengths on place-mat-size paper (giving children a choice of lengths to use in cutting). To make sort mats, draw different shapes (circles, squares, triangles, rectangles) on place-mat-sized paper. Laminate the mats for durability and cleanliness.

3. When it's time to prepare the food, children can use the mats to measure lengths of celery or cucumbers, both of which can be cut in short, medium, or long strips, depending on the line the child chooses. Children can place the foods they've cut up in different sections of the sort mat to keep count of how many they have of each.

Teaching Tip

As with the snack mats (see page 34), use a bleach solution of ¼ teaspoon bleach to 1 quart water to clean the fruit and vegetable mats. (For teacher use only. Use permanent marker to label the container with its contents; keep out of children's reach.)

Oceans Away

Adding an unexpected ingredient can make a recipe special. With this recipe, children will discover just how special when they bring a blueberry gelatin "ocean" to life with gummy fish and other sea creatures.

1. Mix up a package of blueberry gelatin, allowing children to help as appropriate. (They can help, for example, by counting out ten stirs apiece to mix up the gelatin.) Place prepared gelatin in clear cups. (This will allow children to view the "sea creatures" through the side of the container.)

2. As the gelatin sets, have children add a number of edible gummy sea creatures to the mix. Choose a number they can count to, such as five.

3. Have children make number sentences to go with their oceans—for example, "Two starfish plus three fish equals five things swimming in my ocean!" Or "2 starfish + 3 fish = 5 sea creatures."

4. Children can count backward as they enjoy their edible oceans and eat each sea creature: "Five, four, three, two, one . . . no more sea creatures left!"

Digging in Dirt

For a garden version of Oceans Away, make chocolate pudding in clear containers and let children add gummy worms. As the pudding sets, children can add their worms. They can make number sentences related to worm colors—for example, "Four red worms plus one green worm equals five worms in the garden." Or "4 red worms + 1 green worm = 5 worms."

Ice Cream Sundae Party

Create an ice cream sundae counter to culminate a food or restaurant theme and give children a chance to use numbers in an authentic way.

1. Using the order form on page 109, have children indicate how many marshmallows, gummies, sprinkles, strawberries, and other ingredients they want on their sundae. Give children a limit so they can practice counting numbers up to 10 or 20.

2. Use conversation to scaffold children's understanding. For example, if children are counting out ten of an ingredient, help them notice that halfway to ten is five.

3. When children complete their order forms, have them head over to the ice cream sundae counter to create their own sundaes, counting and measuring ingredients along the way.

Teaching Tip

Provide laminated ten frames (page 40) so children can count out up to ten of any particular ingredient. For example, children who want bananas on their sundaes can cut and count out ten banana slices using the ten frame.

Math Talk

Use mathematical language of *more than*, *less than*, and *equal to* as children prepare and compare vegetables. "I wonder" questions work well:

- I wonder how many more red foods there are than yellow. How could we find out?

- I wonder: If we count all of the cups with vegetable pieces, will we get to twenty cups?

- I wonder: If we count by tens to find out how many vegetable pieces are going into our soup, will we go past one hundred?

Note: Children can use numeral cards (page 37) or roll-out graphs (see page 19) to organize objects and answer these kinds of questions.

Name _____ Date _____

 # Build a Recipe

_____ cereal   _____ nuts

_____ raisins   _____ pretzels

_____ dried cranberries   _____ sunflower seeds

_____ dried cherries   _____ other

Name _____ Date _____

 # Tea Party Order Form

Choose one: ## Choose one or more:

_____ white bread   _____ cream cheese

_____ rye bread   _____ peanut butter

_____ wheat bread   _____ butter

                                        _____ fish

                                        _____ celery

                                        _____ apple

Name _____ Date _____

Ice Cream Sundae Order Form

_____ scoops of ice cream

_____ marshmallows

_____ strawberries

_____ gummies

_____ shakes of sprinkles

_____ squirts of whipped cream

Draw a picture of your ice cream sundae.

Integrating Math Into the Early Childhood Classroom   Scholastic Teaching Resources

Movement and Outdoor Activities

Standards Connections					
Activity	Number and Operations	Algebra	Geometry	Measurement	Data Analysis
Line-Up Games	•	•			
Elevator	•	•			
Dressed for the Weather	•	•			•
Sandbox Investigations	•	•	•	•	
Swing Count	•		•		
Plant for Spring	•	•		•	•
Outdoor Shape Hunt	•	•	•		•
Sun and Shadows	•	•	•	•	
How Many From Here to There?	•	•	•	•	•
Snowy Day Fun	•	•	•	•	•
Warm Weather Fun	•	•	•	•	•
Temperature Counts	•	•		•	
Seasons and Change	•	•		•	•

Movement and outdoor activities offer children a chance to unwind, to play with one another, and to use their physical skills to their maximum ability. Some games and activities, such as hopscotch, have math as an essential element. Other activities have embedded math opportunities that can easily be utilized, such as measuring shadows. Physical engagement and motor play should be considered to be of the highest importance.

Line-Up Games

A floor full of feet makes lining up a learning experience every time. Children are active participants in playful problem situations as they listen to directions, pay attention to numbers called, and follow through with corresponding actions.

1. Cut out foot patterns. Make a pair of foot cutouts for each child in the class. On every pair of cutouts, write a numeral. For example, on each cutout of one pair, write the numeral 1. On each cutout of another pair, write the numeral 2, and so on. Repeat numerals as necessary. Laminate if desired.

2. Arrange cutouts two by two on the classroom floor. Line them up so children can see the number sequence. Tape the cutouts securely in place.

3. When it's time to line up, have everyone stand on a pair of feet. Sing an adaptation of "If You're Happy and You Know It"—for example, "If you're on the number five, please clap your hands" or "If you're on the number ten, please stamp your feet." Sing enough variations until everyone has had a chance to participate, then off you go!

Elevator

This elevator game provides practice in number recognition and in early addition concepts.

1. Make a deck of counting cards consisting of the numerals 1, 2, and 3, with multiple copies of each (page 37).

2. Create a mat with the numerals 0–10 arranged vertically, with 0 at the bottom. Allow plenty of space for a couple of children to stand next to each numeral. Lay the mat on the floor or ground so children can walk on it.

3. Explain to children that this elevator will take them to the top floor where they can visit the sticker shop (or any other fun place). Each child takes a turn picking a card and proceeding up the elevator that many floors. Children continue until they reach the top, where they can choose a sticker. As a variation to the Elevator game, add plus and minus signs to the cards, so children can move up or down the building.

In both full- and half-day programs, counting chants at line-up time provide practice with counting while supporting successful transition routines. "One, two, buckle my shoe . . . " is a familiar chant that incorporates mathematical language. You can also clap and tap a sequence (such as, clap your hands, then tap your head as you count one, two, three, four . . .).

Teaching Tip

Dressed for the Weather

When children return from recess on the first cold day, have them bring all mittens and gloves to the circle and create a quick mitten and glove graph by lining them up in two columns on the floor, mittens on one side, gloves on the other (or use roll-out graphs, see page 19). As children explore the data on this colorful graph, they might compare how many pairs of mittens there are and how many gloves, and how many individual mittens and gloves there are altogether. Be sure to post the results of this investigation. Repeat the graphing experience on another cold day and compare results. *Are there more gloves or mittens today? Compared to the first cold day, are more or fewer children wearing gloves? Mittens? Gloves and mittens?*

Sandbox Investigations

A batch of freshly made sand cakes or pies provides many countable moments and opportunities to engage in math conversations as children play.

- Containers of various sizes give children an opportunity to make big cakes and little cakes, five cakes or three cakes. Say, *Oh, they look so delicious! What would happen if I ate three of your cakes? Would you have any left? If I wanted to buy six cakes, how many more would you have to make?*

- Use sandbox investigations to incorporate measuring. Children can use lengths of yarn to measure a sand castle, the length of a big road that runs through the sandbox, or the circumference at the base of a mountain of sand.

- Self-stick tags make convenient labels for items children measure (placing the label on the yarn). Or glue index cards to craft sticks to make signs children can place in the sand to show what they've measured. Adding machine tape is another good measuring tool; make a note directly on the adding machine tape to record the child's remarks about the measurement, including, for example, what was measured (road, mountain, even a "cake") and what the measurement represents (height, length, width, circumference).

Swing Count

For math moments with a physical component, count how many times children pump on a swing. When others are waiting for a turn on the swings, it is a good time to count down from ten until the next child gets a chance to swing. Counting backward helps children develop a mental number line. It improves their recall of the number that is one more or one less than a given number. Counting forward and backward makes number order meaningful.

Plant for Spring

After talking about flowers that grow from bulbs, plant some in the classroom as children wait for spring to arrive.

1. Sort and count the bulbs with children (tulips, daffodils, or other flowers) before planting each variety as directed. Count how many bulbs you plant and record the information on a picture chart for later use.

2. As children wait for the first shoot to appear, mark the time by creating a paper chain for each type of flower planted and adding a link for each day that goes by (or use plastic links). Use a different color for (or place a sticker on) every tenth link to provide children with another way to keep track of time. (They can count days that pass by tens.)

3. Continue to keep track of the days as the flowers grow. This gives children a chance to construct knowledge around the relatively short time it takes to force bulbs. Compare the length of the paper chains. *Which flower took the fewest number of days to sprout? To flower? Which took the most number of days?*

4. When spring arrives (at least in the classroom), compare the number of bulbs planted with the number of flowers that grew.

113

Outdoor Shape Hunt

One day hide a multitude of paper shapes in different colors around the playground. Write children's names on paper bags, then let them go on a shape hunt, placing what they find in their bags. Afterward, children can sort what they found by shape, size, and color. To develop understandings related to exclusive and inclusive sets, they can further sort shapes in a group by other attributes—for example, sorting triangles by color (red triangles, blue triangles, yellow triangles, and so on), or colors by shape (red triangles, red circles, red squares, and so on). Invite children to compare categories—for example, count how many triangles each child found and how many altogether. Another variation is to assign each child a list of shapes to look for and how many of each. Or divide the class into buddy pairs and have each pair look for only one kind of shape.

Sun and Shadows

Choose a sunny day and outline shadows with chalk. Measure them every which way—for example, the length or width of children's shadows or the shadow of a tree, a trash can, or some other object of interest. Making note of the angle of the shadow may be more difficult to convey, but it is certainly interesting for children to see the difference in angle when they return to their outlines. Later in the day, return to your tracings, and let children discover where the shadows have moved:

* *How far did the shadows move in three hours?*

* *Did any of the measurements change?*

* *Can you predict where your shadows may be in another hour?*

How Many From Here to There?

Counting is such a critical skill—practice it whenever, and wherever, possible.

* As the class goes to the gym (or the library, the water fountain, the lunchroom, the playground), ask children to count the steps it takes to get there. To keep everyone on track, tell them that they may whisper as they count. When children become competent they can try counting silently. Try several routes over several days and compare the number of steps for each route.

* Use frequent trips to the playground to investigate ideas related to measurement and distance. Ask: *How many steps do you think it takes to get to each location? Is it farther to get to the swings or to the slide?* Walk with children from the classroom to each spot on the playground. This is a good time to compare and contrast differences in everyone's walking steps. Count and compare steps, and record distances (in steps).

* Use bar graphs to record data. Use discussions about the data to reinforce mathematical language, such as *longer, shorter, farther, closer, most,* and *least.*

Snowy Day Fun

Snowy days are full of math connections to make.

1. Make snow angels. Measure how tall or how wide the snow angels are. One way to do this is to count footsteps from head to toe or from one side to the other. Explore area by counting the number of footprints it takes to fill in a snow angel.

2. After making snow angels, let children retrace their steps and count footprints they made on their way to make snow angels (to practice one-to-one correspondence).

3. Notice other tracks in the snow. Animal prints, such as those of a bird or rabbit, are fun to count. *How many steps did a dog take in newly fallen snow?*

4. Snowmen present a chance to count how many snowballs it takes to make two, three, or four snowmen, and to explore sets. *How many eyes on all of the snowmen?* (Repeat with other features.)

5. Record with words and pictures (drawings or photographs) children's "snow math" discoveries so they can revisit their investigations and add to their understanding.

Teaching Tip

Bring snowy day explorations indoors with *Snowballs* by Lois Ehlert (Harcourt, 1995). Irresistible collage illustrations depict a snow family, complete with a spotted dog. Young readers can continue the counting they started outside to include the snow characters in the book: How many snowballs? How many eyes, noses, and mouths? The book includes factual information about snow and a recipe for popcorn balls (which, of course, invites more opportunities for math).

Warm Weather Fun

Outdoor fun in warmer climates may not include snow, but there are exciting opportunities for active learning.

- Children love collecting shells and stones. Shell or stone hunting can be the springboard for shell sorting and graphing after the hunt is over.

- A warmer climate allows for ongoing flower (or vegetable) garden explorations. From selecting seeds to planting them and tending the garden that grows, there is a lot of math going on. Notice numerals on the seed package. *How deep do the seeds get planted? How many days until they sprout?* Mark it on a calendar. Count days until the plant becomes visible and compare it with the information on the package. Compare growth rates for different flowers (or vegetables).

- Numbered obstacle courses are easy to set up and change to keep children's interest high. Make obstacle-course "station" signs consisting of a picture that represents an action children can perform, such as hopping, touching toes, or bouncing a ball, and a numeral that tells how many of those actions children will perform—for example, "3" hops, "4" ball bounces. (You can also use dots to represent the quantity.) Number the signs to indicate stations in order. Refresh the obstacle course periodically with new actions.

Temperature Counts

Mount a thermometer outside and use it to develop understanding of "higher than" and "lower than."

1. Allow children to examine the thermometer up close to see how temperature is measured.

2. Check the thermometer with children and record the temperature. Notice record-breaking temperatures. It is not essential to track the temperature each day unless that appeals to your students, but rather, establish a high temperature and a low temperature and update them any time a new record is set.

3. Display the record temperatures (highs and lows) in the classroom so children have a visual of the number and degree sign.

"Measurement is one of the most widely used applications of mathematics. It bridges two main areas of school mathematics —geometry and number."

(NCTM, 2000)

Math Talk

Conversations that connect seasons with concrete experiences help children make sense of concepts related to past, present, and future. Following are sample conversation starters:

- When we came to school in the fall, I noticed . . . Now that it's winter, I see . . . What changes have you noticed?

- Soon it will be spring; I think we may see . . . What else do you think we'll see?

- Oh, look! The first flowers are starting to bloom! That tells me spring is really here. What else do you think we'll see?

- Let's count all the hats we see people wearing today. How many do you think we'll count?

- How many people do you think we'll see wearing boots? What do you think this tells us about the weather?

Seasons and Change

Concepts of time and change (including past, present, and future) continue to develop throughout the elementary years. It is helpful to construct an understanding of change in its simplest terms by looking at seasonal changes.

1. Give concepts of change context by counting the number of days to events to find out "how long ago" and "how long until."

2. Use the verses on page 118 as springboards for walking tours to look for seasonal signs. Bring along a clipboard to record children's observations.

3. When you return to the classroom, organize the list by categories, such as animals and plants, and compare: *Did we see more flowers or baby birds?*

4. You can add to the list as each season evolves. New signs are popping up all the time!

Fall

The leaves will fall from trees so tall
When autumn knocks upon the door.
We'll look for signs of fall today;
So many things we'll have to say!

Things to look for:

- Leaves of every color
- Acorns
- Milkweed
- Seeds of flowering plants that may be blowing away
- Birds migrating

Winter

When ice and snow cover the ground,
We'll take a walk and look around
To find the many signs that show
What winter looks like high and low.

Things—some high and some low—to look for:

- Clouds
- Birds
- Icicles
- Imprints in the snow
- Branches of trees
- People wearing cold-weather clothes

Spring

Oh, what fun, here comes the sun,
Time to skip and time to run.
Oh, what fun, today is spring,
Let's look for things spring will bring.

Things to look for:

- Birds
- Flowers
- Buds on branches
- Umbrellas

Summer

When days get hot, we'll look a lot
For signs that summer's really here:
Shady trees, maybe buzzing bees?
What will we find, both far and near?

Things to look for on a beach walk:

- Shells
- Stones
- People
- Birds
- Waves
- Fish

Things to look for on a city walk:

- Birds
- Flowers
- Trees
- People
- Bicycles
- Insects

Home-School Connections

Standards Connections					
Activity	Number and Operations	Algebra	Geometry	Measurement	Data Analysis
Hot News	•	•	•	•	•
Stairs, Stairs, Everywhere!	•	•			
Ways to Go	•				
Picture This	•	•	•		
House Count	•			•	
Tick Tock	•		•	•	
Twos, Twos, Twos	•		•		
I Spy Shapes	•		•		

Research supports the importance of home-school connections. Children whose families are involved in their learning have more success at school. These learning experiences are most effective when they are "real-life" activities in which the math component is an enriching addition.

Everyday life is filled with many teachable moments for families to help children solidify math skills and strengthen confidence in mathematics—from sorting socks to shopping for groceries. When it comes to sorting socks, for example, children can count pairs and even count by twos. A nearby parent or other caregiver can wonder aloud how many socks there are and join in with counting by twos, ". . . two, four, six, eight!" Opportunities abound at the grocery store: *How many kinds of cereal do we see in this aisle? Let's count the fruit in our cart! How*

Have children bring
their send-home
activity pages back
to school so that
you can give them
lots of positive
feedback about
their explorations,
problem solving,
and discoveries.
This gives children
a chance to tell you
how they completed
their pages and
for you to gauge
their developing
understanding.

*many people are in line in front
of us? How many bags do you
think we'll need to pack up these
groceries?*

When families share everyday
math experiences, children
develop a comfort level with math
and a sense that math is useful
and important. The activities in
this section (each a reproducible
"send-home" page) are designed
to help families make these math
connections at home and support the skills being developed at school in effective
ways. Adapt these pages (both the notes and activities) as needed to best meet the
needs of your students. Encourage parents to build on the rich math environment
of school by using mathematical language and engaging in everyday counting,
sorting, and comparing in much the same way that they have been encouraged
to build on the print-rich school environment by reading to their children and
modeling the use of print.

In addition to sending home "investigations" for children to work on with
their families, teachers can build home-school connections in many other ways—
for example:

- Including classroom-based math experiences in weekly or monthly newsletters

- Sharing block-building experiences by sending home adding machine tape cut
  to the exact height, width, or perimeter of a child's building, along with a note
  written directly on the adding machine tape telling about the block building
  and measuring (see page 66)

- Using prepared templates to send home quick notes about individual children's
  mathematical experiences. (pages 24, 38, 66, 67, 121)

- Sending home simple recipes you've prepared as a class for children to share
  with their families and make at home together (see page 101)

*"Graham (1994) explored the
roles of family, culture, and
language on 2-, 3-, and 4-year
old children. In her study, she
found that parental attitudes and
practices greatly influenced the
mathematical development of
these young children."*

(Graham, Nash, & Paul, 1997)

Hot News

Name _____ Date _____

_____ was a super problem solver today.
(name)

Here is the problem: _____

And here is _____ 's solution:

_____

What a super problem solver!

Hot News

Name _____ Date _____

_____ was a careful counter today!
(name)

Here is the number where the counting started: _____

The counting went all the way to _____ .

What a careful classroom counter!

Hot News

Name _____ Date _____

What delightful data ideas _____ shared!
(name)

Here is what we were graphing: _____

And this is what _____ noticed:

_____

Integrating Math Into the Early Childhood Classroom Scholastic Teaching Resources

Stairs, Stairs, Everywhere!

Dear Families,

Each time you and your child climb up or down stairs, there are opportunities to practice counting. The counting skills are important, of course, but so is matching one number to each stair (one-to-one correspondence). If counting begins to feel too easy for your child, try estimating how many stairs there are before you start. Once you know the total number of steps in a staircase, try counting (but not climbing) backward from the total!

Sincerely,

_____

Stairs, stairs, everywhere!
I will count them here and there.
I will count them right outside.
The stairs I climb to get inside,
I will count them to the door.
Inside I will count some more.

1 Are there stairs going into your home? Count them.

There are _____ stairs going into my home.

2 Are there stairs inside your home? Count them.

There are _____ stairs inside my home.

3 Count more stairs.

Where I counted more stairs: _____.

There are _____ stairs here.

Integrating Math Into the Early Childhood Classroom Scholastic Teaching Resources

Ways to Go

Dear Families,

Children will be amazed at your knowledge of numbers if you remember to share what you know! As you and your child are out and about, notice numbers together. There are numbers at the grocery store (numbers at the deli counter, numbers at the checkout, numbers of apples in a bag or eggs in a dozen), numbers at the bank, and numbers at the gas station (how many gallons and price). Try to talk about math and have a hunt for numbers wherever you go. For more number fun, share the rhyme here and count with your child all the ways you can get around town.

Sincerely,

_____

Ways to Go

I count the ways I can go,
Sometimes fast and sometimes slow.

Buses, when their wheels go round,
Take me all across the town.

Roller skates go zipping by.
Ice skates work in wintertime.

Skiing makes my legs work hard.
On stilts I walk in my backyard.

Can you think of ways to go?
Ways that take you fast or slow?

Put a check next to the ways you and your family get around your town. Then count: How many ways do you get around town?

_____ bike

_____ car

_____ bus

_____ train

_____ feet

_____ rollerskates

_____ scooter

What is another way you can get from one place to another? _____

_____

Name _____ **Date** _____

Picture This

Dear Families,

One of the important aspects of geometry is orientation, the way a shape is placed in a given space. Positional words and phrases such as *above, below, next to, in front of,* and *behind* support developing understanding of space and object. Invite your child to make a map of a favorite place. Encourage understanding of spacial relationships by asking questions such as: *What is behind the chair? What is next to the books?*

Sincerely,

_____

A Map of My Favorite Place

Integrating Math Into the Early Childhood Classroom   Scholastic Teaching Resources

Counting Mini-Book

Dear Families,

Children know their home well, making it a good place to count! It is common for children to start counting and just randomly point to objects being counted. As a result the last number counted may not, in fact, be the exact number of the objects. The best way to help children gain this skill is to count along with them for a while or to point to the objects as the child is counting and encourage the child to point with you. Here's a mini-book you and your child can make to practice this skill. Cut out the four pages and put them together to make a book. Then read and complete it together.

Sincerely,

_____

My Counting Book

By _____

In my home, I can count.

How many chairs are all about?

How many tables do I see?

How many people sit with me?

1

How many chairs?

2

How many  tables?

3

How many  people?

4

Integrating Math Into the Early Childhood Classroom   Scholastic Teaching Resources

Name _____ Date _____

Tick Tock

Dear Families,

This activity is meant as a first introduction to the world of clocks and telling time. A clock is a tool that measures time, which may be a new way for children to think about measurement. This exploration is not meant to involve children in telling time. It does, however, offer a chance to investigate the difference between a clock with a face and a clock that shows just the numbers.

Sincerely,

_____

I See a Clock

Two hands go round and round.

They tell me when my bus will come;

They tell me when I'll have some fun.

They tell me when it's time to eat;

They tell me when my friends I'll meet.

They tell me when I sleep late,

Or when I need to rush or wait.

They help me plan each single day—

When it's time to work or play.

Where do you see clocks?
Draw a picture.

Integrating Math Into the Early Childhood Classroom Scholastic Teaching Resources

Name _____ Date _____

Twos, Twos, Twos

Dear Families,

Your child is already learning so much about numbers—right at home! For example, whenever you sort laundry together, your child can match socks to make pairs. Lining up winter boots or summer sandals also teaches about pairs. These kinds of experiences help your child develop understandings about numbers and counting. To do more, try the activity here. As you and your child read the rhymes below and look for pairs of things around your home, practice counting them by twos: two, four, six, eight, and so on. Invite your child to draw pictures of the items you count, too. Have fun counting and exploring together!

Sincerely,

_____

I have socks that are really neat, Here are socks I wear on my feet.	I have boots for rain and snow. Here are the boots that help me go.
I have shoes that help me run. Here are the shoes I wear for fun.	Something else that comes in twos:

Name _____   Date _____

I Spy Shapes

Dear Families,

It is important for children to learn some basic characteristics about shapes to build a foundation for later study in geometry. For example, they discover that all triangles have three sides and that they may be the same length or different lengths. This activity gives children a chance to identify shapes, use shape words, and represent shapes on paper. Use the places identified here for your shape hunt. Cut out each square and glue it to a sheet of paper. Have your child draw the shapes he or she finds.

Sincerely,

_____

Kitchen

Kitchens have a lot of shapes

Like the pans for baking cakes—

Circles, rectangles, or squares?

Look around—they're everywhere!

Living Room

In the living room where families sit

All kinds of interesting shapes fit.

A rug, a chair, or a TV?

Draw the different shapes you see!

Bedroom

Bedrooms are a place to rest,

What shape describes a bed the best?

What other shapes do you spy?

Dresser? Door? A light up high?

Yard or Playground

Look for shapes on the days

That you go outdoors to play.

Swings to ride, games with balls?

Look and draw them, one and all!

Integrating Math Into the Early Childhood Classroom   Scholastic Teaching Resources